Nick Middleton was born in London in 1960. He has a doctorate in geography and as a geographer he has travelled in more than forty countries. He teaches at Oxford University on a part-time basis and has worked as a consultant to the World Conservation Union and the United Nations Environment Programme. His travel and environmental articles have appeared in a number of magazines and newspapers, including the *Independent* and *The Times*, and he has written several books on geographical topics.

By the same author
Kalashnikovs and Zombie Cucumbers

The Last Disco in Outer Mongolia

NICK MIDDLETON

PHŒNIX

A PHOENIX PAPERBACK

First published in Great Britain by Sinclair Stevenson in 1992
This paperback edition published in 1995 by Phoenix,
a division of Orion Books Ltd,
Orion House, 5 Upper St Martin's Lane, London WC2H 9EA

A CIP catalogue record for this book is available
from the British Library.

ISBN: 1 85799 012 9

Printed and bound in Great Britain by
The Guernsey Press Company Limited

CONTENTS

ACKNOWLEDGEMENTS

I am indebted to many people for their help and encouragement during the writing of this book. First and foremost I would like to thank the people of Mongolia, without whom there would be no book. Some of their names have been changed for their own protection. I would also like to thank the following: Adrian Fozzard, Rosie Hadden and Mark Carwardine for their harassment which made me write it; Bulcsu Siklos and Rita Middleton for their support and comments on early drafts; Caroline Robertson for her browbeating; Brenda Bowen for her help with the title; and Amanda Tress for welcoming me home after my first visit. I am also indebted to the British Council and the government of the Mongolian People's Republic who jointly funded my first visit.

I gratefully acknowledge the following books from which I have quoted extracts.

Peking to Paris by Luigi Barzini, first published in 1908. Revised edition first published by Alcove Press Ltd 1972, published in Penguin Books 1986. © Luigi Barzini Jr, 1972.

Asian Odyssey by Dimitri Alioshin, Cassell & Co., London, 1941.

Stanford's Compendium of Geography and Travel, E. Stanford, London, 1906.

The Modern History of Mongolia by C. R. Bawden, 2nd ed., Kegan Paul International, London & New York, 1989.

Beasts, Men and Gods by F. Ossendowski, Edward Arnold & Co., London, 1923.

Mongol Journeys by Owen Lattimore, Jonathan Cape, London, 1941.

Istoriya Dzhunarskovo Khanstva by I. Ya. Zlatkin, Moscow, 1964.

Folk Tales from Mongolia by D. Altangerel, State Publishing House of M.P.R., Ulan Bator, 1986.

Natural History of Central Asia, vol 1: The New Conquest of Central Asia by J. Chapman Andrews, American Museum of Natural History, New York, 1932.

PREFACE

Imagine that you are Tintin, the intrepid boy journalist. You are travelling to some far-off Asian republic in search of an ancient Buddhist scripture that contains a vital clue needed to unravel a plot of international intrigue. You arrive in a small aeroplane with funny markings and Cyrillic writing on the fuselage. As you circle the runway, your travel-weary brain takes in the treeless hills that sparkle here and there with streams apparently petrified like icicles in their channels.

The airstrip is guarded by impenetrable-looking military in khaki uniforms, stars on their epaulettes and fictitious insignia on their lapels. Dotted over the runway are a dozen large troop-carrying helicopters, their five rotor blades drooping like a grasshopper's tentacles. Across the tarmac the terminal building looks rather East European and out of date. As you step out on to the runway, you have to squint because of the bright sun shining from the wide blue sky which is the backdrop. The air is crisp and mountainous.

In the Tintin adventure the country is called Sylvania; in the Marx Brothers film the name is Freedonia; in real life you have just arrived in Outer Mongolia.

I have often wondered why it is that Outer Mongolia occupies such a special place in so many people's minds as the most remote spot on earth, possibly even the last place God made. It is the only country in the world where Queen's Messengers, the intrepid band of British diplomatic postmen, forego their usual solitary routine and travel in pairs.

As Aeroflot flight SU 563 bumped to a halt at Ulan Bator Airport, I could feel my stomach fill with an emotional cocktail of excitement and trepidation, based on half a gallon of cheap Russian red wine that a Bulgarian geologist had been pouring down my throat ever since we had left Moscow nine hours before.

While waiting for my connection at Sheremetyevo Airport I had shared a couple of beers with a small party of Moscow-based journalists, two French, an American and two Japanese. They had been as excited as I was about visiting this fabled Central Asian country, although they looked at me sideways when I told them I would be staying for two months. The journalists travelled business class (or was it then Party class on Aeroflot?) and were met on the runway to be whisked away in a jeep. I flew economy class, squashed next to the Bulgarian with whom I conversed in broken French in the stuffy drunken atmosphere thick with smelly Russian cigarette smoke. There was no one to meet me on the runway.

I walked into the terminal building clutching my passport and visa. Two very orderly queues, of the sort only encountered in England or an Eastern Bloc country, were beginning to form in front of the small glass booths where entry stamps were being thumped on to passports and travel documents. My Bulgarian acquaintance burped loudly as I asked him to help me fill in the landing card. It was printed in Russian and Mongolian, neither of which

x

I had mastered beyond the cursory 'hello's and 'thank you's. I had been told in London that I would get by in Mongolia with a smattering of Russian, but that people would not necessarily take very kindly to me if I did. The Berlitz *Teach Yourself Russian* tape had confounded me in the first four minutes, and, although that international bastion of travel and linguistics runs to an Urdu and Afghan tape, they have not, as yet, marketed a Mongolian course.

As far as I knew my papers were in order, but they were in Mongolian and thus totally incomprehensible to me. The people at the London embassy might have typed 'professional spy' under the occupation section for all I knew. The British Council briefing in London had been rather disorganised in the way the British Council seem to have perfected. No one really seemed to know what I should expect. But one point that had been made several times was that Mongolia is very definitely a Soviet satellite state and that bugging and police surveillance should be accepted as part of the Mongolian way of things.

Forewarned is forearmed, of course. I had had enough experience of Asian authorities to know that give a man a uniform and some power and it invariably goes to his head. Transiting through Moscow some years before, I had realised that the Russians have also devised an excellent game plan for exasperating arriving passengers. The passport check is conducted by two teenage soldiers ensconced in glass boxes suspiciously like the ones I was now queuing for. The teenage power brokers looked at each passenger in turn to decide just how long we were to be kept waiting. I got ten minutes I remembered, during which time the beefy figure in the box either looked straight at me or straight through me, but mostly he gazed into a middle distance just past my left ear. My time up, he paid attention to the documents on the counter in front of him and with curled lip did the necessary rubber stamping.

My turn came. The young Mongolian in the glass box did not look mean. He took my passport and papers and stamped them. Obviously he had not been fully trained yet.

I collected my suitcase and approached customs. The customs man spoke slow but good English, took a quick look through my hand baggage and asked whether I was carrying any offensive literature. I hoped that a copy of yesterday's *Times*, some short stories by Pushkin and my collection of academic papers on soil erosion would not qualify. He smiled and waved me through. First two rounds to me.

There were no marauding taxi drivers battling for my favours in the arrivals hall. In fact no one took any notice of me at all. The scene was very orderly. Most of the passengers on the flight had been Europeans and as they emerged from customs they were met by their colleagues or loved ones and disappeared through the swing glass doors. The occasional Mongolian wearing a long padded wrap-around outfit that was a cross between a dressing gown and an overcoat, tied at the waist with a brightly-coloured silk sash, wandered in and out of the terminal building.

I had been told that someone from the University would be at the airport to meet me so I took up position near the door casually flicking through the pages of my British passport hoping that I would be immediately recognised as the English specialist they were waiting for.

No one came. Ours was the only flight of the morning and gradually everyone disappeared. A cleaner began emptying the ashtrays. Behind the counter at the far end of the short hall the two customs men giggled loudly. This would never happen at Sheremetyevo, the airport staff training programme must be a long way behind schedule.

Still no one came. Arriving at almost any other world capital I would be armed with a guidebook of sorts, a map of the city, a short list of cheap hotels to aim for and an idea of by how much I should expect to be ripped off for a taxi ride to get there. But this was Outer Mongolia. No guidebooks, no map, no notion of where a hotel might be and apparently not a taxi in the entire capital. I looked for a telephone, despite the fact that I had no Mongolian money to put in it and no hope of being understood. It did not matter because there are no public telephones in Mongolia.

One of the immigration officers came over to lock the doors. I asked her if she could ring the University for me. The woman smiled through her thick-rimmed glasses as she pulled off her tie. She remembered that there had been someone to meet me yesterday, but yes she would ring. As I sat waiting in the deserted hall the giggling customs men came over. They asked if I had seen the Beatles and suggested we go to lunch together. We left my luggage in a small office and moved upstairs to the staff restaurant. Lunch was a thick meat soup called *bantan* which my hosts assured me in another fit of giggles was very good for hangovers. Some cold lamb, canned vegetables and a few thin chips followed. It was washed down with a glass of cherryade. I had no Mongolian money and they paid. This genuine friendliness from the two hungover giggling Mongolian customs men seemed grossly at odds with the Communist military state I had been expecting where minders and tapped phone calls were the order of the day. These men took their work seriously but there was an air of innocence that one might expect of people whose parents, like generations before them, were probably nomadic herdsmen. It was an impression that was to be reinforced during my weeks in Mongolia.

The country has developed quickly since 1921, when the revolutionary leader Sukhe Bator rode into Mongolia with a Soviet Red Army back-up. From that date the country has embraced Communism, and in doing so has necessitated a rewrite of the Marxist-Leninist textbooks, because the pre-revolutionary country had never left the 'feudal' state. Thus, the phrase that lingers on the lip of every Mongolian interpreter was born: Mongolia had 'bypassed capitalism'. It is this rapid shift from old to new that gives today's Mongolia its mystical air as a sort of People's Republic of Shangri-La.

Three hours passed before the University people eventually arrived. They had experienced great difficulty in commandeering a car to drive them the mile or so to the airport. Ulankhu, an electronics graduate, introduced me to a man from the Meteorology Department, who looked rather uncomfortable in his mackintosh and pork pie hat, clutching a leather briefcase. We climbed into the battered taxi and the woman driver gunned the vehicle into action. The handles to open the windows were broken and the clutch made an ominous grinding noise when the driver changed gear.

The drive into Ulan Bator was a journey through a time warp. Just outside the airport a Chinese-looking gateway straddles the road and the Cyrillic script on the large hoarding beside it proclaims the entrance to the city. But as we drove through the arch the view all around was the same one of grassy treeless hills with not a soul in sight.

As we rounded a bend the outskirts materialised. The grass plains were carpeted with compounds of tents. These were of the round felt variety, which, as Ulankhu explained, are called *yurts* by the Russians but *gers* in Mongolian. Kids with crewcuts played in a dried river bed in front of the tents.

The palisades of *gers* faded into an area of Dickensian factories spewing acrid smoke into the mountain air. There were few cars on the wide roads as we approached the centre of town: lines of faceless apartment blocks and drab buildings, an East European clone on the wild Central Asian setting. The taxi pulled up outside my home for the next eight weeks, the Hotel Ulan Bator.

The Hotel Ulan Bator is the best hotel in Outer Mongolia. It is one of only two in the capital where Westerners are allowed to stay. It used to house the French Embassy and is the watering-point for visiting trades union delegations and track-suited athletes from all over the Eastern Bloc. The entire hotel, like all Mongolian buildings, smells powerfully of meat fat. 'Dear guests,' its trilingual brochure announces, 'we are at your disposal.'

I soon found myself in Room 303, a rather palatial suite that consisted of a bedroom and attached bathroom and a sitting room with two sofas, a TV and fridge. It was not unpleasantly decorated, the furniture in a wood the red colour of pecan nuts.

I opened the windows, double frames against the bitter continental winter, and surveyed the city. Across the park outside the hotel the valley hills were fading fast at the end of the day. The neon sign on the building opposite flickered into life. In my Western ignorance I imagined it to be advertising a shop. Later I discovered it said: 'Let's make our capital a good socialist city.'

I pulled from my pocket a small Novosti Press booklet, printed in English, that I had picked up in the airport. It was one of those ubiquitous propaganda publications that socialist countries seem to delight in producing, entitled *Mongolia and the Soviet Union: Sixty-five Years of Friendship and Co-operation*. At the back there was a short questionnaire to fill in on the merits of the book. The questions were answered by ticking one of a series of four boxes labelled 'excellent', 'good', 'could be better', and 'hard to say'. I thought I might use their incisive system to assess my first few hours in the Mongolian People's Republic. After not much consideration I decided that it was 'hard to say'.

Three years later I stood surveying the same view. Mongolia was apparently little changed. Ulan Bator still retained a *Marie Celeste*-like air which hung like a shroud over the capital, built in the middle of nowhere, a concrete centre which the people did not really know what to do with. The wide grey concrete streets were the same colour as the strips of dead grass that bordered them and the red neon letters spelled out the same tired message concerning the socialist city. But the appearance disguised the fact that Mongolia in 1990 was a very different place from the one I had been in three years before.

In a sense this is a 'before and after' book. By the time of my second visit the winds of change that blew through Eastern Europe at the end of the 1980s had rustled the grass of the Mongolian steppe. The Communist dictatorship whose rule had been directed from Moscow for the previous sixty-nine years had suddenly found itself alone and had yielded to domestic pressures for a more open and democratic society. Mongolia is waking up from its long history of domination by foreign powers. It is probably fair to say that today the country is looking forward to a future which will be more autonomous than at any time in the seven centuries since Genghis Khan, their national hero who has been resurrected from a shady Communist past, to be revered once more as a symbol of truly Mongolian independence.

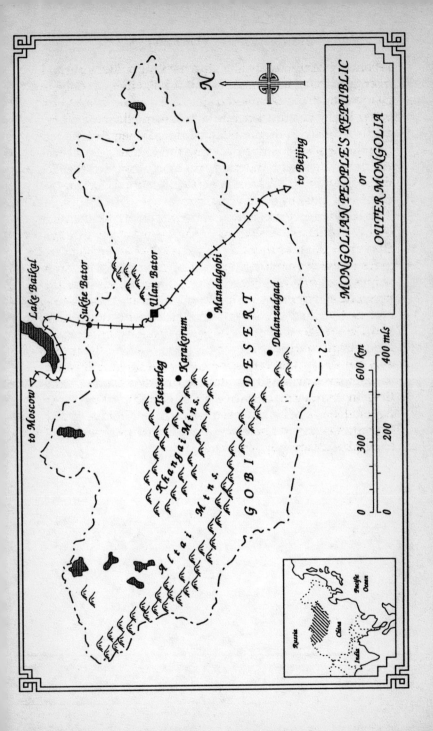

. 1 .

THE UNSUCCESSFUL
PSYCHOPATH

Ulan Bator used to be a nomadic city. Every few years, when new pastures were needed for the animals and new fuel supplies for the stoves, the tents would be dismantled and loaded on to horse and camel to be taken to a new site. But gradually the city grew so large that it stayed put in the valley of the River Tuul where it stands today.

The city took root in the latter half of the eighteenth century. At that time it was called Urga. Shortly after the Communist revolution in the 1920s, the name was changed to Ulan Bator, or 'Red Hero'. Since then it has been the capital of the Mongolian People's Republic and has rapidly grown to become a metropolis of half a million inhabitants. It is by far the largest city in a country the size of France, Spain, Portugal, Italy, Austria and Switzerland combined. A country which is home to just two million people.

Although most of Ulan Bator's population still lives in

gers, times are changing. Slowly but surely the neat rows of tents that hem in the city on all sides and are laid out like a pimpled overlay on the foothills of the surrounding valley slopes are being cleared and the people of the steppes rehoused in faceless apartment blocks.

When Guy Hart, the British Ambassador at the time of my first visit, arrived in Ulan Bator, his flat in the small embassy building overlooked a *ger* compound. While I was in the city, he found himself facing a wasteground; today it is a concrete block.

It is all in the name of progress, of course. In their drive to modernise the country the Socialist Construction Team targeted the *ger* as an unwanted reminder of their feudal past. Not surprising really, since the round felt dwellings have changed little in the 750 years since Genghis Khan and his deconstruction team swept out from the Mongolian steppes to conquer the largest empire the world has ever known. Genghis himself had a high-tech *ger* that could be moved about on wheels, pulled by twenty-two Mongolian oxen. The last ruler of Mongolia before the Communist revolution lived in a *ger* covered with the skins of a hundred snow leopards. The head of state before democratisation, a President whose name was Batman, resided in a Soviet-built concrete palace and was driven around in a black Russian Zil.

Certainly the apartment blocks must be a modern improvement for the lives of the average Mongolian: no *ger* has hot and cold running water or toilet facilities. But at the same time it is sad to have to note that the Soviet-style town planning authorities seem to have mastered the uncanny knack of making every building look drab, monotonous and boring. A quick glance down Peace Street, for example, provides the same vista as that taken in during yesterday's stroll along Lenin Street or, for that matter, the long haul up Stalin Street that is just coming to a thankful end.

While the modern buildings that line Ulan Bator's paved

streets represent 'progress', the cost has been high. The socialist city of Ulan Bator has lost virtually all its oriental character and mystique. The colour and life of the place has been drained out of it. Some of the pre-revolutionary descriptions of Urga paint a quite different picture, of a place now gone for ever. Luigi Barzini, a journalist on the *Corriere della Sera* in Milan, passed through Urga in 1907 with the Italian Prince Scipione Borghese on an epic car journey from Peking to Paris:

> We caught rapid glimpses of courtyards encumbered with packing-cases, with camels, with children; of Chinese buildings with railings of a complicated geometric design, and of little, showy, many-coloured temples. Behind the primitive defence of these hoardings we saw the signs of prosperity and labour. The inhabitants here are all given to trading on a large scale. They are enriched by the commerce of tea, wool, fur and horses. They are regular organisers of caravans, owners of hundreds of camels and oxen.

A European traveller in the 1920s gives a similar impression of a lively, colourful city divided into distinct sections, although it was already a place where the modern world had begun to make an impact:

> No town in the world is like Urga. Upon us new-comers it made an extremely strange impression. The most conservative eastern life and customs exist side by side with western innovations like the telegraph, the telephone and motor-cars. The houses of the Russians cluster around a church with Byzantine cupolas. Colossal Buddhist temples rise high over thousands of felt-covered Mongol tents. Mounted Mongols, slippered Chinese, long-bearded Russians and smiling Tibetans swarm between palisaded compounds whose walls are hung with gaily fluttering prayer-flags. At the eastern

3

end lies the *mai-mai-ch'eng* of the Chinese [the Chinese sector], a complete fragment of China in whose innumerable shops the sons of Han offer their wares to the Mongols riding by.

On the dusty, filthy market-place, yellow and red lamas, their pointed headgear wreathed with roses, swing prayer-mills in their hands as they hurry about among mounted nomads clad in the splendid, parti-coloured robes of the many different tribes. Caravans of camels rock forward through the narrow winding lanes. Dogs prowl everywhere.

The majority of today's inhabitants of Ulan Bator wear style-less Western clothes. The lamas, temples and prayer flags have all but disappeared, and the camel caravans have been replaced by motor vehicles and the Trans-Mongolian Express train. When Luigi Barzini and the Prince Borghese sped through the streets of Urga in their 1907 Itala, the Mongolians marvelled at their cart that must have been pulled by an invisible winged horse. The admiring crowd wanted to know how close they could stand to the sacred mystery without being in danger. But the wide-eyed innocence of the steppe people has gone, and urban modernity has almost engulfed their traditional way of life as they have striven for the socialist panacea.

This is not to say that the Urga of old did not have its unpleasant side. Many visitors to the city remarked on the filth and garbage:

The streets were so dirty and smelly that men had to use special narrow paths for communication. In addition, the streets were infested with numerous vicious-looking dogs. It was extremely dangerous to go out without a special stick with a sharp iron point. A horrible spectacle was presented also by the Mongolian custom of tossing dying people into the streets to be devoured by the dogs. The 'sanitars of the city' would encircle the half-dead person waiting patiently for his last agonies to cease, before commencing their feast. A body untouched by dogs was considered to be rejected by the gods. However, such cases were extremely rare.

But the vibrant, almost medieval city of religion and international commerce, whose streets were bustling with Mongol, Buriat and Tibetan riders, Chinese and Russian traders just seventy years ago, is dead and gone. Its *raison d'être* as a centre for pilgrimage and religious teaching, and trade with its settled neighbours to north and south, has been ripped from its heart because these things were incompatible with Communism. In its place is a sterile, characterless city with about as much style as a military parade ground.

Most of today's trappings of a modern urban society have been presents from other Communist states, who had been eager to give a leg up to their Central Asian partner in cultural crime and, at the same time, no doubt, to have the opportunity of offering an all-expenses-paid trip to the edge of the world to any recalcitrant engineers and construction crews who might need a timely ideological refresher course, well away from the temptations of the wicked witch of the capitalist West. The Hungarians built the water-purifying plant and the fairground big wheel. The Chinese, before they fell out with Moscow in the 1950s, built many of the older apartment blocks and the city's only department store, appealingly named The Big Shop. It was some time into my first trip before I was told a joke that goes around the small Western circle in Ulan Bator. A visiting trade union delegation, after a tour of foreign-built factories and housing compounds, asked: 'And what have the Mongolians built?' The answer is that the Mongolians have been building socialism.

My first few days in the capital were spent sorting out the details of my work programme. I had been asked to set up a wildlife adventure holiday for a new British tour company. My hosts were Mongolia's largest environmental organisation, the Mongolian Association for the Conservation of Nature and Environment. This was my second visit to the country. Three years before I had arrived in Ulan Bator to study dust as a doctoral research student. (In 1982, just having embarked upon my thesis on dust, I was struck by a small red notice on a board in the bowels of Oxford's Bodleian Library. The notice advertised British Council-run research trips to Outer Mongolia. The idea appealed immediately and I duly applied. When permission was eventually granted five years later I had completed my thesis, but the prospect of a trip to the land of Genghis Khan was too good to turn down.)

The capital still had the atmosphere of a permanent building site. Few vehicles drove the streets of Ulan Bator. Every other one was khaki, usually a jeep, with an occasional civilian bus. Every fourth person was in military uniform, some Mongolian, some Russian. But as if by magic the taut atmosphere of repression that I felt keenly in 1987, though it was seldom expressed in so many words by Mongolians, had disappeared. In its place was a sense of energy and alertness, a great reawakening from the deadpan, crushing burden of Soviet domination. Mongolia in 1990 was rediscovering its roots. The Yellow Hat Buddhism, long repressed by the Communists, was flowering once more. Genghis Khan, whose somewhat unsavoury techniques of warmongering had not exactly endeared him to the authorities, was being resurrected as a great leader of men and a Mongolian who was proud to be just that. Mongolians the country over were standing up and speaking their minds in the heady atmosphere of post-perestroika freedom of speech. Three hundred years of Manchu rule and sixty-nine years of Soviet imperialism had suddenly vanished and Mongolia was once more a place for Mongolians to decide what was what.

This transformation was immediately evident when I sat down to lunch at the Hotel Ulan Bator with the men from the Environmental Organisation. My mentor was a man named Tserendeleg. Mongols essentially have only one name. Occasionally an initial appears before that name but it is fairly irrelevant. The precursor Mr was also rather inappropriate among Mongols, I always felt. Tserendeleg was not Mr Tserendeleg but simply Tserendeleg. He was a smiling middle-aged gentleman in a suede jacket and a beret worn at a jaunty angle.

'We have experienced many changes since your last visit to our country,' he explained through the interpreter, a fresh-faced youth with rosy cheeks. 'We have made many mistakes, but we realise this now. There is much work to do to put things right.' He smiled. 'There are now many parties in Mongolia,' he explained, 'soon we will have democratic elections. All parties have said they will introduce a market economy to our country. Before, our economy approximately belonged to the Soviet Union, but now we are independent. We want to enjoy better relationships with the West. This is why your visit is timely.'

We discussed my travel plans. The simple fact that it was apparently possible for me to visit any part of the country was a transformation from my first trip when travel outside the capital had been well-nigh impossible. The ideological differences that had been a continual source of aggravation had also evaporated. I remembered all too clearly the verbal combat I had enjoyed three years before with one of the interpreters, a woman named Tsetseg.

Tsetseg was a secretary and translator at the Mongolian Institute of Hydrometeorology. She was a pretty woman who always dressed in rather smart Western-style suits. If she had owned a string of pearls, she could have been described as a Mongolian Sloane. There was a major drawback to working with her: she had very bad breath. Every time she opened her mouth a strong odour of rotting meat bore testament to the fact that toothpaste is not easy to obtain in Mongolia.

Tsetseg was married but had no children yet, though this was a clear priority since Mongolia needs all the people it can get, she told me. She was gentle and kind but a devout Party woman. Between our sessions of talks with a stream of experts who told me about the climate, drought, rainfall and winds in Mongolia, Tsetseg would probe me about the condition of the peasants in England. A number of times we almost came to blows over our ideological differences in the panelled board room where I worked beneath a stern-looking portrait of the revolutionary leader Sukhe Bator in national costume. Tsetseg had been educated in Moscow and knew how things were organised in the capitalist world. She was not impressed by my blatant lies about free schools and a National Health Service. I was obviously a puzzling specimen. Over the previous five years I had written several times to the Institute to enquire after the possibilities of my visiting them. None of the letters had ever been answered. Tsetseg had opened them.

'I remember you have written many letters in past years,' she said one day.

'Yes,' I replied.

'But why you write more times?' she asked inquisitively. 'Your first letter is received by us.'

Mongolia's harsh continental climate means that the landscape is a parched brown for ten months of the year and only for a brief summer spell does the steppe turn into a rich green carpet awash with the colour of edelweiss and purple gentians. A woman at the University once asked me, with furrowed brow: 'Is it true grass always green in England?'

But then the general ignorance in Mongolia of the British scene is no less informed than the average Brit's knowledge of things Mongolian. Genghis Khan is probably the only Mongol anyone has ever heard of, and probably the best-known in history. Unfortunately for him, he is more renowned for his rather brutal *modus operandi* than anything else, and it is this undesirably barbaric image that made him an embarrassment to the socialists in charge of modern Mongolia. Certainly there are some horrific stories of death and destruction wrought by Genghis and his hordes of nomadic horsemen. The heads of unfortunate victims were piled into pyramids, with separate rows for men, women and children; prisoners were sometimes boiled alive in an iron cauldron; and strong young men captured in one town would be used as an expendable vanguard for the march on the next. As one biographer of Genghis Khan puts it: 'In the early years of their rise to power under Genghis Khan, the Mongols had no idea of the social function of a town. All they knew was to plunder and destroy it and massacre its inhabitants.'

It was not so easy in the thirteenth century to conquer the largest empire the world has ever known without employing bloodthirsty tactics. The vast numbers of innocent people who were dispatched and the enormous destruction wrought were only unusual, during those days, in being on such a large scale. At its height the Mongol Empire stretched from the River Danube to the Pacific Ocean; there were not enough Mongols around to control such an area with an occupying force, so terror was the order of the day.

Besides, it was not just the enemy that bore the brunt of Mongol atrocities. They had developed some interesting methods for executing their own folk. For princes and other people of high rank it was forbidden to spill any blood, so strangulation by bowstring or asphyxiation

9

under a pile of carpets were particular favourites for dealing with wayward royals. It was also not unusual for the entire family to be dealt with in the same way since wives and children were often considered accessories to the crime.

But despite, or because of, the bloodletting, Mongol society itself was quite peaceful during the days of the Empire. An envoy sent to one of Genghis Khan's successors in 1245 by Pope Innocent IV was impressed by the absence of fights, brawls, wounding and murder and the lack of large-scale thieving and robbery among the Mongols. But at the same time he was rather horrified at some of the less salubrious aspects of Mongol society such as the fact that drunkenness was not only commonplace but considered honourable. All in all, John of Plano Carpini considered the Mongols to be a sly, deceitful, cunning and dirty lot who ate only meat. 'They consider the slaughter of people nothing,' he exclaimed and went on to detail how, during one siege, the city's inhabitants held out for so long that the Mongols themselves ran out of food and resorted to eating every tenth man in their own ranks. 'In short,' he concluded, 'it is impossible to put down in writing all their evil characteristics on account of the very great number of them.'

As the *Stanford's Compendium of Geography and Travel* of 1906 puts it: 'The first thing which strikes the traveller in the life of the Mongol is his excessive dirtiness. He never washes his body, and very seldom his face and hands. His clothing swarms with parasites, which he amuses himself in killing in the most unceremonious way.' The complete absence of any form of hygiene among the Mongols is simply explained. Since the rare springs in their arid land were representatives of higher powers, water was not allowed to be fouled on religious grounds. Therefore no washing of the body, clothes or cooking utensils could possibly be undertaken.

Genghis Khan was a brilliant tactician who built and

ruled an empire based on an outstanding level of discipline and organisation. One particularly impressive aspect of this organisation was the mounted courier service, known as *Yam,* that Genghis Khan established to keep him in touch with developments in the far-flung corners of his Empire. Along the routes covered by couriers, staging posts were set up where riders could obtain fresh horses, food and rest, while between these official posts all inhabitants of the Empire were obliged to put the interests of the *Yam* before their own. Approaching riders announced their arrival by ringing a bell, so that a new mount could be made ready. For particularly important messages, riders could cover 300 miles in a day. To do this they first had to wrap themselves tightly in strips of silk to prevent the shaking of internal organs which could easily result in death. As a consequence, riders could not eat *en route*.

And what of the rest of Mongolian history? The great Empire lasted only a hundred years or so. In 1368 the Mongols were expelled from China, but the fleeing Emperor and his descendants continued to be in charge of what became the Chinese Northern Yuan dynasty for nearly 300 years. Then it was the Manchus who took over, ruling Mongolia in a pragmatic way, allowing the Mongols to get on with things but at the same time letting Chinese traders penetrate and eventually run the country. Indeed, for the last two centuries of Manchu rule Mongolia to all intents and purposes became mortgaged off to the Chinese merchants. Individual Mongols and regional administrations known as 'banners' fell into debt all too easily. In extreme circumstances the cunning Chinese merchants were able to extract payments by threatening suicide, since under the law of the times anyone who drove another to suicide could be held accountable for his death.

Not a lot is known about goings-on in Mongolia during the last hundred years of Manchu rule. In the words of the eminent British Mongolist, Professor Charles Bawden:

11

'There can be fewer blank pages in the history of the civilised world than the story of Mongolia during the nineteenth century.'

Then, in the early dawn of the 1900s, after centuries of foreign domination, Mongolia briefly tasted her independence once more. In 1911, when the Manchu Ching dynasty finally fell to bits, the Mongols proclaimed their independence and found themselves a monarch in the guise of the Living Buddha of Urga, the Boghd Khan, the eighth reincarnation of a line of Buddhist gods whose ancestors are traced back through time immemorial. Although the Boghd Khan was a fairly pragmatic living god – he was to die blind, riddled with syphilis – he was revered by all Mongols in the way only a living god can be. Initially the Boghd Khan's sovereignty was limited to the eastern parts of today's Mongolia. The western areas were still occupied by Chinese forces who were eventually routed by Mongolian armies led by a character who was typical of that troubled period in Mongol history between the fall of the Manchus and the establishment of Communist control.

The man in question was known as Dambijantsan, a very able leader with serious magical powers (he was a specialist in gun magic) and probably the reincarnation of a rather evil spirit. He rode a snow-white horse, wore a large white cape and was followed wherever he went by a white dog with red eyes. Dambijantsan has been portrayed as both hero and anti-hero, but, whichever way he is described, it involves some horrific cruelties.

People who offended him had their eyeballs removed. This was done by placing sheep's knucklebones against the outside corner of each eye and slowly forcing them in as a cloth was tightened behind the head. The bulging eyeballs were snipped free with a pair of scissors and Dambijantsan kept them, with others similarly obtained, tucked under the felt covering of his tent. There are also stories of him skinning captives alive, though not while conscious, and dedicating his war banners in the ancient Mongolian way by smearing them with the blood of human hearts ripped from the chests of living Chinese prisoners. The seats of honour in his tent were said to have been covered with human hides.

The story of Mongolia in the early years of the twentieth century is littered with tales of such psychopaths. Perhaps the most deranged of all was a White Russian named Baron von Ungern-Sternberg, who briefly held power in the 1920s after Mongolia had once more slipped back into the role of occupied territory.

The declaration of Mongolia's independence in 1911 had encountered a problem: it was ignored. The one treaty the Mongolians were able to sign was with Tibet which recognised their independence, but that hardly mattered. The reality of Mongolia's position between the Dragon and the Bear was evident when just two years later the Sino-Russian Accord of 1913 reduced Mongolia to an autonomous region of China. By 1917, as Russia rumbled with internal strife, China cancelled Mongolia's autonomy and moved in to occupy the country once again. This time it was short-lived. The Chinese had not reckoned with Ungern-Sternberg, the 'Bloody Baron'.

Baron Roman Feodorovich von Ungern-Sternberg was a professional military man from a long line of soldiers of fortune that was descended from Attila the Hun, so he claimed. His ancestors had taken part in the Crusades and throughout history they had been feared fighting men: Baron Heinrich, a wandering knight, was nicknamed the 'Axe', and the eighteenth-century Baron Wilhelm was referred to as the 'Brother of Satan'. True to family tradition, Roman Feodorovich had a glittering military career in the Russian army, rapidly rising to the rank of Major-General by the age of thirty-three and winning the coveted Cross of St George on the way. But although undoubtedly a courageous fighter, his fearless aggression had not been bridled completely by military discipline. When he entered a café, the other customers usually made a hasty exit, since the Baron was an expert with his gun and had slain many a fellow officer during his excessive drinking bouts.

Truth and legend about the Baron have become indistinguishable during the course of time. The few descriptions of the man do not agree on the colour of his eyes or hair, but they all paint the same picture of a madman on the loose. A Polish geologist who spent some time with the Baron after the capture of Urga describes him as having:

> a small head on wide shoulders, blond hair in disorder, a reddish bristling moustache, a skinny exhausted face like those on the old Byzantine ikons. Then everything else faded from view save a big, protruding forehead overhanging steely sharp eyes. These eyes were fixed on me like those of an animal from a cave.

An officer who served in the Baron's band describes him as:

> tall and slim, with the lean white face of an ascetic. His watery blue eyes were steady and piercing. He possessed the dangerous power of reading people's thoughts. A firm will and unshakable determination possessed those eyes to such an extent that they suggested ominous insanity. I felt a cold shiver run up my back when I saw them. He had unusually long hands and an abnormally small head resting on a pair of large shoulders. His broad forehead bore a terrible sword cut which pulsed with red veins. His white lips were closed tightly, and long blond whiskers hung in disorder over his narrow chin. One eye was a little above the other.

While still in Russia Ungern-Sternberg had been converted to Buddhism and thereafter his excesses were driven by a religious fervour. When the Bolsheviks rose to power he saw them as the realisation of the unknown curse mentioned in Buddhist and ancient Christian books. He immediately set about founding an order of Military Buddhists 'for the struggle against the revolution' as he put it, 'because I am certain that evolution leads to the Divinity and revolution leads to bestiality'.

Ungern-Sternberg's selection procedure is described to us by an officer in his army:

> He would stop at each man separately, look straight into his face, hold that gaze for a few moments, and then bark: 'To the army', 'Back to the cattle', or 'Liquidate'. All men with physical defects were shot until only the able-bodied remained. He killed all Jews, regardless of age, sex or ability. Hundreds of innocent people had been liquidated by the time the inspection was closed.
> . . . His Buddhist teachers taught him about reincarnation, and he firmly believed that in killing the feeble people he only did them good, as they would be stronger beings in their next life.

In establishing his order the Baron introduced celibacy among his followers in line with the teachings of the Yellow Faith. At the same time, however, 'in order that the Russian might be able to live down his physical nature', as he said, he introduced the limitless use of alcohol, hashish and opium.

Although the Order of Military Buddhists never really took off, the Baron did succeed in gathering about him a small force of three hundred ferocious men, and it was this army that was driven from Russia and entered Mongolia in 1920.

The Baron had a simple plan of action as he galloped across the Mongolian border. He was going to establish a new pan-Asiatic state, centred in Mongolia and incorporating Tibet, the motherland of Buddhism, and Manchuria.

Having established a Mongolian Empire, he could then invade Russia and exterminate the hated Bolsheviks. With this aim in mind, it was not surprising that Ungern-Sternberg also believed that he was the reincarnation of Genghis Khan himself.

So it was that Mongolia was taken by the scruff of the neck by a band of psychopathic renegades under the leadership of an insane military leader. The story of Ungern-Sternberg's attack on Urga in February 1921 is told in graphic detail by one of his officers, Dmitri Alioshin, in his memoirs. As his men awaited word from the Baron on when to launch the attack, they whiled away their evenings by the camp fire discussing the pros and cons of necrophilia. The Baron, being a religious man, was advised on the timing of the assault by his personal band of diviners and soothsayers. After days of hanging around in the sub-zero temperatures of the Asian steppe, the attack when it came was not a pretty sight, but the carnage after their conquest was worse:

> Mad with revenge and hatred, the conquerors began plundering the city. Drunken horsemen galloped along the streets shooting and killing at their fancy, breaking into houses, dragging property outside into dirty streets, dressing themselves in rich silks found in the shops. . . . It was remarkable that nobody paid the slightest attention to their wounds; whether the excitement was too great or they had become used to cuts and bruises, I do not know . . . the mob attacked Jews, and all of them perished in the agony. The humiliation of the women was so awful that I saw one of the officers run inside the house with a razor and offer to let the girl commit suicide before she was attacked. . . . The drunken mob invented a new sport of killing men on the streets by striking them direct in the face with thick wooden blocks. There was one Cossack who was killing his own men right and left, until he was shot himself.

16

Kadet Smirnov chose to strangle old women, because he enjoyed seeing them quiver under the grip of his fingers as he broke their necks.

After three days and nights in a bloody nightmare, the Baron called a halt and set about reorganising Mongolia. Urga was cleaned and disinfected; he introduced currency and paper money, set up a cabinet of ministers, arranged a city bus system, built bridges and re-opened schools. Having liberated the Mongols from the hated Chinese and once more put the Boghd Khan on the throne, the Baron was hailed as a hero and saviour.

But it was not long before the Baron's popularity faded. The man who could devise such penalties for insubordination as lowering the offender into a large fire from a tree, or pouring turpentine into his rectum, struck terror into the hearts of his new-won people. His sidekicks were no better. Colonel Sepailoff, who was made Commandant of Urga, joked and sang while he executed people. 'He was always nervously jerking and wriggling his body and talking ceaselessly,' explains one observer at the time, 'making most unattractive sounds in his throat and sputtering with saliva all over his lips, his whole face often contracted with spasms.'

The Baron's personal adjutant, a man by the name of Teapot, was also a demented animal. He was always present when the Baron gave an interview. If during the course of conversation the Baron requested a teapot, the man would cautiously slink behind the guest, suddenly grab him by the neck and strangle him to death.

The poor Mongols soon became weary of their savage occupiers and bewildered at the Baron's apocalyptic speeches incorporating quotations from Buddhist scriptures and the Revelation of St John. In less than a year the insane dreams of Ungern-Sternberg were dashed. His band of cutthroats lost control of Urga after they had ridden off to wreak havoc against the Bolsheviks in Siberia.

Their disorganised and ill-disciplined rampages were quickly defeated by the more professional Red Army. The Mad Baron's troops mutinied, broke up and tried to shoot him. A vivid description of Ungern-Sternberg in his final days shows he was near the end of his tether:

> He had lost his hat and clothing. On his naked chest numerous Mongolian talismans and different charms were hanging on a bright yellow cord. He looked like a reincarnation of a prehistoric ape-man. People were afraid to even look at him.

Eventually the Baron was captured by a Red Army patrol. On 13 September 1921, *The Times* reported that he was being exhibited 'as a monster' at the stations of the Trans-Siberian railway en route to Moscow for trial. But, in fact, he was already being tried at Novosibirsk in Siberia. He was found guilty on every charge, all of which carried the death penalty. Defiant to the end, the Baron refused to accept the 'people's court', denying none of the charges and declaring to the court that his thousands of victims had only got what was coming to them because they were 'too red'. On 15 September 1921, the Baron was put before a Red Army firing squad and shot.

When news of his execution reached Urga, the Boghd Khan held a memorial service for the reincarnation of Genghis Khan. To the accompaniment of bronze cymbals and huge drums, a last prayer was said for Baron von Ungern-Sternberg.

But unfortunately for Mongolia, worse was yet to come. The Baron's evil reign had provided just the excuse the Red Army needed to ride into Mongolia and set up its first satellite state.

· 2 ·

REAL MEN DON'T EAT VEGETABLES

The opportunities for having a good time outside work in Ulan Bator are rather limited. Places to eat other than the Hotel Ulan Bator and its rival the Bayangol are very few and far between, and by all accounts only to be visited if one is interested in contracting curious diseases. I never came across anything resembling a bar, and the only cinema in town existed solely to project Soviet propaganda films which I would not understand anyway.

One evening during my first visit Tsetseg arranged to take me to the State Opera House, where the resident ballet company was performing Tchaikovsky's *Swan Lake*. We would be accompanied by the Head of the Institute's Foreign Relations Section, a busy man named Dembereldorj who spoke good English and had travelled outside the Communist world.

I met Tsetseg and her bad breath on the steps of the

19

Opera House as the sun was beginning to sink below the hills behind the city.

'Dembereldorj is absent,' she told me in a scolding voice, as if it were my fault. We waited a while, Tsetseg stamping her feet on the wide steps and becoming not a little agitated. Filing past us was the evening's audience, many military officers in their peaked caps and heavy coats and a couple of busloads of Russian civilians.

'Dembereldorj not here. Why is he absent?' she exclaimed for the fourth time as we moved into the theatre.

The dancing was not first class and the orchestra not the best but it was a good evening's entertainment nonetheless. On leaving the theatre, at which Dembereldorj had continued to be absent throughout, I could not help asking Tsetseg what the young people of Ulan Bator do for kicks.

'They stay with their family,' she replied. 'They help the mother and tell themselves stories.'

One of the joys of foreign travel is to observe and participate in the way of life of the local inhabitants. But for reasons of state paranoia, communicated to the people through an active network of secret police and their informers, a visiting capitalist in 1987 was not invited into the average Mongolian home to enjoy their hospitality. A walk through the streets of the city was certainly an eye-opening experience the first couple of times, due to the eerie quality of emptiness and drabness, but the initial excitement of being in such a bizarre and to me little-known place soon wore thin. The potentially more interesting compounds of *gers* surrounding the concrete centre were, I was told, out of bounds. And, besides, while I was in Mongolia in early spring the sun set rapidly at around 6 p.m. and most of the time the temperature was well below the mark at which brass monkeys begin to suffer.

The transformed atmosphere of the city during my second visit was therefore confirmed one day when Sainu, the fresh-faced translator, asked me to dinner at his flat. His apartment block was situated on the wide Avenue of Leisure that ran from The Big Shop to the modern round building housing the State Circus. It was a short walk from the temporary offices occupied by the Environmental Organisation behind a library known as the Young Technicians Palace. The palace was crowned by one of the ubiquitous neon signs.

'What does the sign say, Sainu?' I asked him as we left.

'Embarrassing,' he replied, and continued walking; he was obviously not going to tell me. I stopped and tried to decipher the Cyrillic characters for myself.

'It is old-fashioned sign,' Sainu said at last. 'It says "Long Live Marxism-Leninism".'

'Communist bullshit,' I replied. He did not know the word, so I had to explain it to him.

'Yes,' he said satisfied. 'It is old Party bullshit, no longer necessary in Mongolia.' He enjoyed the new word and repeated it to himself over and over as we approached his flat.

The apartment was a standard one, apparently. There was a small kitchen, a toilet and three other rooms. Sainu was in his mid-twenties and married with a little baby, and he and his family shared their accommodation with an assortment of in-laws. His wife was a handsome woman named Nara who had very long silky black hair. They had been married for just over a year.

When at school, Sainu had been one of the brightest boys in his region or *aimak*, and so he had been chosen to take the examinations for college in the Soviet Union. He had passed with flying colours and opted to go to journalism school in Leningrad. True to form, however, the bureaucratic machine managed to enrol him in Moscow on a five-year course in International Law. Protest was useless, he was on the list for law and that was all there was to it. It was a worthless qualification, he told me. What chance is there to practise Soviet international law in Mongolia? he asked. Particularly now that the country is busy translating legal texts from the West so that it can furnish itself with a non-Soviet system?

Hence he had returned to Mongolia with a smart-looking certificate qualifying him to do nothing. He had dabbled with the idea of becoming a Buddhist monk but had fallen foul of a policy change at Mongolia's then only working monastery in Ulan Bator. He had been with the Environmental Organisation for nine months and at last some of the skills learnt at college were being put to use, although it was only his knowledge of English. This was his first assignment as interpreter for a foreign visitor, and so far he was quite enjoying it, he said.

We were joined for dinner by Tserendeleg, the organisation's vice-president, and Sainu produced a bottle of *arkhi* – Mongolian vodka – so that we could toast my arrival and the hope of a profitable collaboration. On Sainu's suggestion I had purchased a bottle of whisky from the 'dollar shop', Tserendeleg's favourite brand, White Horse. The Mongolians are obsessed with the idea of toasting and we soon ran out of excuses so started once more on the same ones as before. By the time the food arrived, we had finished the bottle of vodka and started on the White Horse.

The fare was fried pastry parcels with chopped meat inside, a plate of which was constantly replenished by Sainu's wife who did not join us to eat. Tserendeleg was in high spirits, glad to relax a bit after a hectic few weeks. Everyone was working hard towards the elections which would be held in less than two months' time. He himself was a Party member, but I was surprised when I learnt that Sainu, like most of the younger generation, did not support the old Party. There seemed to be no animosity between them. The feeling appeared to be very much one of healthy respect for each others' opinions.

Tserendeleg was keen to explain some aspects of Mongolian life as the White Horse began to take effect. He proudly told me that he had been the first Mongolian to visit Antarctica some years before. He had spent a year there as part of the international scientific effort on the southern continent. He was very proud of the fact that he had proved the hardiness of Mongolians since the sub-zero temperatures and long periods of isolation had affected all other nationalities more than him. Life in Mongolia had prepared him well. His country had a healthy climate, he told me. The very severe winters, in which temperatures of minus 30 and minus 40°C are commonplace, mean that there is a sort of annual cleansing of disease and bugs which cannot survive these harsh conditions. It seemed to make good sense.

Mongolian bodies and social habits had also of course developed according to these conditions.

'Many foreign visitors believe Mongolians are dirty people,' he said, 'but no washing is necessary during winter months because the Mongolian body does not sweat. Our customs are just different from yours because we do not need to wash regularly.'

Tserendeleg asked me how I thought Mongolia compared to other developing countries I had seen. There were similarities and differences, I told him. Mongolians were poor in a material sense relative to the British, but not as poor as in many countries. I had never seen a homeless Mongolian, for example, and no one here was starving or reduced to begging on the street.

'Ulan Bator is a typical Third World city,' I thought, 'in that it is so much larger than any other Mongolian town.' About one-quarter of the country's population, half a million people, lives in the capital, while the next largest city has a population of just 75,000. 'But Ulan Bator is not congested like most cities in developing countries,' I said. 'There are not many cars on the streets.'

Tserendeleg nodded. Most Mongolians were not used to city life, he said. People who moved to the city from the countryside found it difficult to sleep at night inside apartment blocks, and many suffer from nosebleeds when they first begin to live within concrete walls. Ulan Bator also had some serious environmental problems, he told me. Air pollution was particularly bad during the winter when the *gers* round the city had their fires burning all day and the two power stations at one end of the valley were busy pumping out clouds of smoke. Unfortunately, the power stations had been located by their Soviet builders perfectly to maximise the pollution effects from the highly sulphurous brown coal that they burnt. They are at the western end of the Tuul valley, and, since the prevailing winds in Ulan Bator are from the west and north-west, their fumes hang in a semi-permanent haze over the city. Ulan Bator was experiencing the effects of acid rain which he thought was damaging plants and possibly animals. Pollution from the factories at the western end of the valley had also killed off many of the fish in the River Tuul. These were just some of the problems that Tserendeleg hoped could be ameliorated with help from the West.

● ● ●

The prospective boredom of the long Mongolian evenings during my first visit to Ulan Bator had been relieved somewhat after I had made contact with another, the only other, British Specialist, as we were so grandly termed in Ulan Bator. I had briefly met the man at the British Council meeting a month or so before leaving for Outer Mongolia. He was of Hungarian descent and had a totally unpronounceable name that sounded like Butcher Shitloss. He had a face that appeared to have been made from rather too much putty, with podgy fingers to go with it. He looked like the sort of person who had a rather miserable time at school.

My initial reaction at the London meeting had not been a favourable one. Butcher Shitloss moaned a lot, came across as a touch on the arrogant side, and was more or less determined to dislike Mongolia whatever happened. As I sat in his suite in the Hotel Ulan Bator, plush and similar in layout to mine, my first impressions were confirmed.

'I was rather pessimistic in general about actually getting any work done in Mongolia before I came,' moaned Butcher, whose reason for being in Ulan Bator was to study Lamaist texts for his Ph.D. 'I mean they're all a bit embarrassed about this kind of thing, you know? They are for ever coming up with reasons why I *can't* see these things.'

He had some justification. He had been here a week longer than I had and had not even been able to find out what was in the library that might have been of interest to him. The faceless wall of bureaucracy had got Butcher down and he was convinced that Mongolia was a nowhere place where there is nothing to do except drink and smoke Camel cigarettes.

'It's a banana republic without the bananas,' he said despondently.

Butcher and I got to know each other well during our stay in Ulan Bator. After a few weeks together I even admitted that I still did not know what his name was.

'Don't worry,' he said, 'no one in Britain ever can grasp it. You probably think it's Butcher Shitloss.'

I smiled.

'I got quite used to this kind of abuse at school. I was heavily into animals and not treading on ants and that sort of thing and suffered accordingly. The name is Bulcsu, pronounced "Bull-shoe", Siklos, "Shick-losh".'

Bulcsu did not really like being 'abroad'. His dislike of things Eastern in general was based on an unhappy year spent in Japan at the University of Nagoya. The fact that Mongolia was a Communist state was also unfortunate.

Bulcsu's parents had fled Hungary after the 1956 uprising, and consequently his opinion of the Communist system was almost pathological in its hatred.

'Let's face it,' he would say, 'most of these Communists are just a bunch of thugs. They weren't elected and needless to say nobody wants them. The only way they can stay in charge is by inflicting a reign of terror.'

He particularly despised the sort of people he came across all too often in the student bars in London where he was studying: those who wore small red enamel badges of Lenin on their lapels. They were often the same people who held all-night vigils outside the South African Embassy or jumped up and down at the latest military clampdown in Chile. It was not that the people in charge of such countries were not also 'a bunch of evil bastards', he explained, but why were the enamel badge brigade not demonstrating outside the embassy of the Soviet Empire about Siberian forced labour camps?

'Where were they when the Russkies invaded Afghanistan?' he asked. 'Nowhere. They weren't there. That was all right because they were socialists.'

Bulcsu was the archetypal academic, passionately interested in almost everything. I could envisage him in thirty years' time encased in a room full of books, peering through his small round glasses. His interests spanned far and wide, from anthropology to religion, to philosophy, to mathematics and physics. His room at home in west London sounded like an Aladdin's cave of bizarre information. He could boast books on the tensile strength of fruit alongside manuals on lake morphometry, volumes on Shamanic rites among Siberian tribes and a gamut of phrasebooks from out-of-the-way places. His favourite in the latter category was one from the Andaman Islands in the Bay of Bengal. On the first page of the book was the Andamanese for the question, 'Why did you let the syphilitic woman tattoo him?', clearly an important everyday enquiry in the life of the Andaman Islands.

We spent many an evening consuming the Western delicacies available in the small dollar shop in the hotel. These amounted to alcohol (*arkhi*, whisky and Cinzano), Cadbury's chocolate, Wrigley's chewing gum and cigarettes. We never actually bought the chewing gum. The sticks were used as small change in the shop. One stick was worth five cents. It transpired that on the streets of Ulan Bator chewing gum was considered a great delicacy, a forbidden fruit from the capitalist West, and that people would pay as much for a stick as one tugrik (about 25 cents). It might have turned into a profitable sideline if the tugriks had been worth anything. As it was there was very little to spend them on, other than lunch and dinner in the hotel restaurants.

The meals in Mongolia were never anything to write home about, unless it was an urgent plea to the Red Cross to send food parcels. There were two restaurants in the hotel, a large hall on the ground floor that had a four page menu on which ninety per cent of items were never available, and a rather smarter room on the second floor that overlooked a statue of Lenin in a park. The smart restaurant served the same food as in the hall but its tables were adorned with linen cloths and small plastic flags of Communist countries.

Mongolia is no place to go if you are a vegetarian. Meat has always been the mainstay of the Mongol diet. Back in the thirteenth century the Franciscan monk William of Rubruck commented that Mongols 'eat all dead animals indiscriminately'. In those days this meant everything that could be hunted and killed: mice, marmots, rabbit, dog, deer, wild pig, rats, antelope, wild horse, cattle and sheep. Usually the meat was boiled or roasted and the leftovers were kept in a leather bag for later, but in emergencies the flesh was eaten raw after a few hours beneath the saddle of a horse that was ridden until the meat was tender. This was a method that the Mongolian chefs at the Hotel Ulan Bator were obviously not familiar with. The dead animals that they prepared were invariably hard and stringy, but perhaps they had kept the meat for themselves and served up the saddle instead. It came in disappointingly international forms and flavours: beefsteak, schnitzel and occasionally fried chicken. There was also a traditional dish of mutton soup-cum-stew called *hoitzer*, the source of the ubiquitous meat fat smell that pervaded the entire city.

It is only in recent times that vegetables and fruit have been consumed in Mongolia. Rice imported from Vietnam, potatoes and cabbage often now accompany the meat. But the older generation in Mongolia ridicule the young about their diversified diet which now includes vegetables. 'Grass is for the animals,' they say, 'and meat is the food for man, and if you eat grass, you will not have a strong body.'

Owen Lattimore in his book of *Mongol Journeys* during the 1940s tells of how he introduced some dried vegetables into a pot of gazelle stew in the steppes one day. He thought the stew a great success and asked his Mongol companion how he had enjoyed this approach to cooking and the vegetables all the way from America. 'Fine,' said his friend. 'Excellent, but let's not have them again. Constipating stuff, vegetables.'

Now and again, Bulcsu and I found some variation in our diet at the student hostel just around the corner from the Hotel Ulan Bator. In the hostel foreigners are given a self-catering room each – a much better deal than the Mongolian students who are crammed six to a room. Secretly, both Bulcsu and I were happy that we had landed the hotel accommodation rather than the hostel. On the one hand, it meant that we would not have to go through the rigmarole of buying live chickens at the market, wringing their necks, plucking and cooking them – something our upbringing along the meat counters of Sainsbury's had not prepared us for – and, on the other hand, it meant that we were obviously thought of as British Specialists and thus something rather more important than common or garden students.

The student hostel had that unfinished air of a building site, although it was obvious that no construction had taken place there for years. Paint was peeling from the whitewashed walls of the four-storey building and the dusty entrance walkway was strewn with rubble. In the middle of the small courtyard was the most extraordinary sight. Radiating out from a central concrete circle was a series of crazy golf courses in complete disrepair. Goodness only knows where you would rustle up a few golf clubs from in Mongolia.

The first evening Bulcsu and I visited the hostel we climbed the stairs to the second floor and presented ourselves to the track-suited Mongolian woman at a shabby desk. As in the hotel, each floor is presided over by a sort of 'floor hostess' whose job it seems to be to sit behind a desk and hinder anyone who wants to do anything as outrageous as walk along her corridors.

'Norbu,' said Bulcsu.

The woman looked blank.

'Norbu,' Bulcsu explained again, and gestured up the stairs to where we knew the Tibetan student named Norbu had his room.

The woman turned her head and threw a quick glance up the staircase as if she had suddenly been confronted with two roving specialist language teachers who had dropped in to give her a crash course in the English word for 'stairs'. She looked blankly at us again and said '*Niet*', the Russian for 'no', a word that all Mongolians in minor positions of power, such as floor hostesses and shop assistants, have learned to use with devastating effect. Her eyes wandered back to the screen of a television set on the other side of the landing. It was surrounded by a dozen or so students, all in track suits and all from North Korea. They were engrossed in what I assumed to be a comedy programme, judging from the laughter and

29

chuckles coming from their ranks. I followed the floor hostess's gaze and looked at the TV set. The programme was showing graphic footage of a seal cull in the Arctic.

'Norbu,' I repeated to the floor hostess, but she had lost interest. What possible use could the English word for 'stairs' be to her?

We walked past her. The floor hostess was on us in a flash. *'Niet,'* she said as another gale of laughter came from the North Korean seal-clubbing enthusiasts.

'Norbu,' we exclaimed in unison. 'We've come to see Norbu.'

From behind us one of the North Koreans appeared, said something to the floor hostess and disappeared up the stairs. The woman motioned us to wait. A minute later Norbu appeared down the stairs and ushered us up. I looked at the floor hostess, but she was lost again in the Arctic.

Norbu was a Tibetan from India. Like many Tibetans of his generation – he was not sure how old he was, but it was around twenty-seven – he had never been to his own country. He wanted to study medicine, but had not been able to get a place at an Indian university; it is not easy if you are a Tibetan refugee. So here he was at university in Outer Mongolia. He had been here for two years already, learning Mongolian and Russian, and had another six to go when he started the medical course. Norbu was quiet and humble to begin with, like many people from the subcontinent I have come across, but he soon warmed up when we described our difficulties with the floor hostess. He was very gentle and had an infectious giggle.

We had been invited to dinner and Norbu made us some tea as he busied himself with preparing the meal. We would be eating porridge, he announced with a broad grin. Bulcsu and I looked at each other with raised eyebrows.

Norbu's room was long and small. He had several posters on the wall, like students' rooms the world over.

The view from his window, which he kept open to let in some fresh air to offset the stuffiness of the well-heated hostel, looked over one of the university departments. The building was old, peeling and dusty looking. On Norbu's bookshelf were several volumes of medical books in Russian and English and one or two more general books on Mongolia. In front of these was a small statue of Buddha in the lotus position.

Bulcsu picked one of the books from the shelf. It was in English and entitled *Bypassing Capitalism*.

'Great book,' announced Bulcsu as he sat on the bed and leafed through the pages. 'Listen to this for a reasoned explanation of why the socialists did away with the Mongolian alphabet: "In the final analysis, life demonstrated the expediency of using the Russian alphabet."'

'Life demonstrated the expediency?' I repeated.

'Sure,' replied Bulcsu. 'What he means is that if you didn't change to Cyrillic they shot you. Really very simple.'

We both laughed but Bulcsu had not been joking. We asked Norbu if anyone still used the Mongolian alphabet, a vertical curvaceous script adopted from the Uighurs by Genghis Khan in the thirteenth century.

'Only old people now,' Norbu told us. 'In schools only the Cyrillic is taught.'

This was just one example of the many ways in which Russian dominance of Mongolia had exerted itself and gradually eroded the Mongolian heritage and culture. Apparently the President before Batman had tried to go one further and ban the Mongolian language altogether, getting everyone to speak Russian. Fortunately, enough nationalist feeling had made itself clear and the proposal had been withdrawn, but no doubt the idea would resurface at some later stage.

Dinner was served and the porridge turned out to be quite different from the Scottish variety we had been expecting. It was a bowl of tasty thick meat stew with noodles. We were joined for our dinner cross-legged on the floor by an Afghan student named Ahmed. Ahmed was an awesome character in running shorts and a vest – the room was very warm and Bulcsu and I had removed several layers of clothing by this time. Ahmed had a strong chest, piercing brown eyes, a wild hairstyle and a handshake like a scrawny vulture.

'Me speaking very little English,' Ahmed explained, but it was more than our Afghan. He looked as fierce as any Afghan tribesman you could ever hope to meet, the sort who would probably not think twice about skinning you alive if you offended him. He gave me some idea of the difficulties the Russian troops must have been facing in his country as we sat around eating Tibetan porridge in Outer Mongolia.

We chatted in English about the Russian influence in Mongolia. Norbu told us he could take us to see the Russian military camp, tucked away up a side valley, and there was a gold mine on the outskirts of Ulan Bator from which the refined gold was flown out to the Soviet Union every night on a special jet. There were perhaps 100,000 Russian troops in Mongolia, so an academic at the university had told him. Another figure I heard later was 75,000. A higher figure still accounted for the many Soviet 'advisers' in the country. It is impossible to confirm, but some believe that at one time during the 1960s there were close to three million Russians in Mongolia, half as many again as the country's entire population. There was no doubt that Mongolia was run from the Kremlin to all intents and purposes. The course of socialist development here had been a very close replica of the Soviet experience, even down to the Mongolians coming up with their own version of Joseph Stalin, a man called Choibalsan who had purged many of Mongolia's remaining Buddhist monks in the 1930s.

Ahmed clearly did not think much of modern Soviet imperialism.

'Russians not good,' he announced, 'no like in Afghanistan,' and he spat on the floor.

But for the wild Afghan the Russians in Mongolia did serve some purpose. Ahmed was a bit of a lady's man.

'Russian womans like good Afghan fuck,' he declared, apropos of nothing, with a graphic gesture using his hand and arm. 'Me no got Kalashnikov,' he continued, 'this my good Kalashnikov,' and he patted his crotch.

In his own little way Ahmed was doing his bit towards undermining the Soviet Union's grip on his country: he impregnated as many Russian advisers' wives as possible.

After dinner Bulcsu and I arranged to meet Norbu the following day so that we could walk to the Soviet zone of the city. We took a long route back to the hotel. The temperature was well below zero but the cloudless sky offered a spectacular array of stars to wonder at.

The evenings spent at the hostel were sanity-saving diversions from the otherwise colourless social life we led in Ulan Bator in 1987. They also made up for the almost total lack of social contact we had with Mongolians. There was, however, one notable exception to this rule.

Bulcsu and I had been whiling away a Saturday afternoon searching his room for evidence of surveillance. The staff at the British Embassy had told us that our telephone lines were certainly tapped and that there were probably various other bugs somewhere in our rooms. Our suspicion had been further aroused a day or two before, when we found the 'floor hostess' from our landing supposedly cleaning our rooms, a previously unheard-of task for someone in her elevated position.

Our search was conducted in a rather lighthearted mood. Bulcsu was no stranger to the atmosphere of East European espionage, having heard numerous horror stories from his Hungarian parents, but he dismissed them since we were British subjects and unlikely to come across anything more unnerving than a tapped telephone. But at the same time neither of us was totally complacent since we had both read stories of innocent victims of such regimes who had no doubt started out with the same confident attitude. Nevertheless, it was difficult to take a State militia seriously when it was headed by a character called Batman.

We had moved all the furniture to the middle of the room and started to look underneath the carpets when Bulcsu's telephone rang.

'It's probably the secret police asking us to check the connections when we do find the bugs,' Bulcsu quipped. He picked up the receiver.

'Hello. . . . Oh hello Bold, yes, yes I'm fine.'

A smile came over Bulcsu's face as he listened to his interpreter on the other end of the line.

'Er, well, don't you think it might be a bit, um, awkward, Bold. Awkward. Er, difficult. Yes, difficult.'

A slow explanation was barely audible.

'Yes, I know.'

More explanation.

'Sure. Yes, I understand that. It's difficult for everyone. . . . OK, I'll come. At three o'clock. OK.'

He put the receiver down.

'That was Bold.'

'What did he want?'

'*Arkhi*.'

It seemed to us either a very stupid or rather suspicious act for Bold to ask for *arkhi* over the telephone in the hotel with the bugging so uppermost in our minds. Bulcsu looked worried. But then again, Bold was all right. He could not possibly be. . . . Could he . . . ?

Once doubt is sown in your mind, you start suspecting everyone of being a security man. Let's face it, I argued, our minders must be sanctioned by the security forces to come into contact with Westerners. But then, we were always being approached for *arkhi*. Every time we went to one of the dollar shops or to the Russian shop for which Bold had managed to obtain a pass for Bulcsu, there were various Mongolians hanging around outside trying to press fistfuls of tugriks into our hands to buy a bottle. It was totally illegal to do it, of course, and we had been warned that some of these attempted transactions were militia set-ups for unwary foreigners.

But then the situation for the poor Mongolians was pretty desperate. *Arkhi* was difficult to come by. They could only buy it on three days a week from their shops, and even then it was not always available. Furthermore, it cost the earth. At seventy tugriks a half litre, this was the equivalent of a week's wages for one of the waitresses in the hotel restaurant.

Bulcsu yielded. He decided to take a bottle wrapped in a newspaper to Sukhe Bator Square at three o'clock, but he was not very happy about it. Then the phone rang again.

'Hello.'

It was a different voice on the line.

After a short conversation Bulcsu replaced the receiver. It had been a man who said his name was Altangerel, a writer, he said. He had heard that Bulcsu was in town and wanted to meet him for a chat. He had just invited him to dinner that evening.

We looked at each other.

'It's the KGB,' I said, only half joking, 'they probably want to ask you why you've been turning your room upside-down.'

Bulcsu was not amused.

I said: 'Did they ask you to bring a bottle of *arkhi*? Perhaps it's the KGB Ball and they're short of guests.'

Bulcsu was flustered all afternoon. We had lunch together in the hotel restaurant, but the sour-faced waitresses would not let us eat in our usual place because all the tables were being used for a trade union conference and were specially laid. The centrepiece of each spread was a magnificent orchid which we were told had been specially flown in from Vietnam for the occasion. We were relegated to the end of the hall where we sat watching the fat trade unionists being treated like kings on the other side of the glass partition. This was usually the Mongolian section, and we had a taste of the resentment some of them must have felt. To cap it all, both the schnitzel and the beefsteak, the usual staples, were off. We had to make do with stroganoff, which was very stringy indeed.

'The condemned man ate a hearty stroganoff,' I joked, but Bulcsu told me it was not funny.

At three o'clock Bulcsu made the *arkhi* run to Sukhe Bator Square. Beads of sweat were forming on his forehead as he pulled on his heavy topcoat, but a few minutes later he returned slightly triumphant. Now there was only the mysterious dinner invitation to worry about.

Altangerel had arranged to meet Bulcsu outside the main post office at the corner of Sukhe Bator Square. We could not decide whether this was suspicious or not. It might be innocent, but if this was a legitimate dinner invitation and this Altangerel character was able to take foreigners into his home, then why would he not pick Bulcsu up from the hotel which was only five minutes walk from the post office? We had both seen too many spy films in which innocents are bundled off the streets and into cars and driven to secret rooms with blank walls for a bit of interrogation. Bulcsu was not attracted by the thought of spending some time in a Mongolian jail. Having seen what their idea of five-star hotel customer service was like, the imagination had to work overtime to conjure up images of Mongolian prison conditions.

A visitor to the old Urga prison in the 1920s described it as 'one of the most horrible prisons in the world'. It consisted of a few rooms that were piled with wooden boxes four foot long by two-and-a-half foot high. These coffins were the prisoners' cells. Some of the poor wretches wore heavy chains around their necks and had both hands manacled together. They could neither sit up nor lie at full length, and their food, 'when the jailor remembers to give them any', was pushed through a six-inch hole in the coffin's side.

After much consideration Bulcsu decided that he would after all meet his mysterious host, but I was to tail him at a safe distance just in case. The precaution was probably ridiculous, but we were not entirely sure.

A small man in a black topcoat shook Bulcsu's hand outside the post office and they headed off down Peace Street. I followed on the opposite side of the road about a hundred yards behind, feeling like George Smiley. After twenty minutes they turned into one of the blocks of flats and I strolled back. It was 7 p.m. The sun was very bright and I was much too hot in my sheepskin coat.

Some hours later I was quietly tucking into a plate of schnitzel and cold chips in the hotel dining hall when the KGB victim reappeared. Rather disappointingly, Altangerel had turned out to be a perfectly legitimate writer and Bulcsu had passed a peaceful evening with no interrogation or thumbscrews. But he had been subjected to a peculiarly Mongolian form of social torture instead, in the guise of three bottles of beer. Mongolian beer is the worst in the world: it smells of animal fat and tastes like a blend of rancid mutton soup and fermented yak's droppings. It was also very hard to come by, of course, in the same way as the *arkhi* was, so as the honoured guest Bulcsu had to swallow every drop of the prized offering and look happy about it.

Altangerel had given Bulcsu a small volume of Mongolian folk tales that he had translated into English. It was full of little stories such as the following, entitled *Seven Mice*.

Once upon a time, there lived seven brother mice. They owned as much land as the palm of a hand. One day, when a handful of snow fell on the ground, the seven brothers were clearing it away and they found some butter as big as an anklebone. They gave it to the youngest mouse to keep, but he licked it up and ate it. So the other six brothers beat him to death.

Then they went to a lama and told him about this deed:

'There were seven of us.'

'You have a large family.'

'We have as much ground as the palm of your hand would cover.'

'You have a big piece of ground.'

'One day a handful of snow fell on our ground.'

'That sounds to me like a disaster.'

'We seven brothers cleared it away.'

'You all worked hard.'

'While we were clearing away the snow we found some butter as big as an anklebone.'

'You became rich.'

'We gave it to the youngest brother to keep, but he licked it up and ate it.'

'He is a good storekeeper.'

'The six of us beat him to death.'

'That was almost war,' the lama answered. And he paid absolutely no attention to them. The six mice had come to the lama to get a decisive answer, but they didn't. They were very disappointed and they knew that the lama didn't know anything and was a fool. Also, they repented their mistake very much, that they had done the wrong thing in killing their youngest brother.

We never did find out just who Altangerel was.

· 3 ·

REACH FOR THE
REVOLVER

To say that Mongolian Buddhism has taken a bit of a
pasting in the years after the Revolution is an understate-
ment: it was almost totally annihilated. At the dawn of
the socialist era the country could boast an estimated 700
big monasteries and over 1,000 small ones. In 1921 there
were some 113,000 monks in a total population of 650,000.
One in every two adult males was a lama of some description and every family wanted to get at least one of its
sons into the church. The monasteries ran the political,
economic and spiritual affairs of the country. In short they
were the lifeblood of Mongolia.

It should therefore come as no surprise to learn that the
Communists, when they assumed power, decided to do
away with them. How could Mongolians be cajoled into
being good socialists if their hearts and minds were fully
occupied with religious nonsense? Hence the destruction
of the church became the first priority in the building of

the new Marxist-Leninist state. The Communists certainly made a pretty thorough job of it. By the end of the onslaught, Mongolia was left with just one functioning monastery and around 200 monks.

It took a little time to get down to the task. For three years after the Revolution the Communists tolerated Mongolia's supreme Buddhist personality as a nominal Head of State, but when the so-called 'Living Buddha of Urga' died in 1924 a decree was issued forbidding the search for his next reincarnation, and Mongolia was proclaimed a People's Republic. There then followed a campaign of harassment. Monasteries were taxed heavily to curb their wealth and the movement of lamas was controlled by administrative regulations.

In 1928 policy became more aggressive towards the church. The strings were being pulled by Stalin's cronies in the Comintern, the Moscow-based body responsible for the spread of international socialism. In Russia, Stalin was starting a new period of revolution in which the Russian Orthodox church was one of the principal targets. Since Mongolia was firmly in the pocket of the Comintern, they too embarked upon a new approach to what they called the 'Lamaist question'. This involved new and arbitrarily high taxes on both monasteries and individual lamas and the confiscation of land and animals from the church. The confiscations were part of the drive towards the collectivisation of animal herding, which had also been dictated from Moscow. Monasteries which could not or would not pay the new taxes had their highest-ranking priests thrown in jail and were visited by carloads of friendly People's Revolutionary Army personnel who paid their respects by burning books, destroying artefacts and vandalising buildings.

The result of this assault on both the church and the economic fabric of the countryside – all private enterprise was also abolished at this time, leaving the country without any transport or shops whatsoever – was open rebellion and civil war. It is a measure of the extent to which Mongolia's rulers had become alienated from their own people that the popular uprising took them completely by surprise. The rebellion was put down by government forces in 1930, only to break out again in 1932. This time the Soviet Army was called in to restore order, which from the church's point of view involved widespread executions of lamas suspected of active involvement in the rebellions.

After these unsettling events, policy towards the monasteries was relaxed. Again Stalin's guiding hand was evident; a message of thanks for his counsel in 1932 praised him for his 'open-hearted and wise advice'. Murder and vandalism were replaced with further legislation. It became illegal to build new temples, ecclesiastical law was terminated and the subordination of one monastery to another was abolished. This last measure spelt doom for poorer monasteries who had long relied on support from larger neighbours to survive. The taxation laws were also strengthened, further squeezing monks out of their temples. Some became liable to pay more in their supposedly income-related taxes than they earned.

Since this nonviolent phase of the anti-religion drive was also a direct imitation of Stalin's internal policy towards the Russian Orthodox church, it again comes as no surprise to find that when Uncle Joe began his all-out assault on the USSR's population in 1937 it gave the green light for a similar programme in Mongolia. The Mongolian authorities also had an excuse, if they needed one, in the form of an increasing threat from the Japanese, whose army had been prodding the Mongolian borders in the south in 1935 and 1936. The possibility that the Japanese might be seen by the church as their saviour, as indeed they probably were, was too good an opportunity to be missed. A 'Final Solution' was put into action.

In 1937 the Party ordered seventy-five monasteries in the Gobi Desert to be relocated at least a hundred kilometres away from the border. Although this may seem a rather mild measure, it effectively meant their closure since the temples had long occupied the only habitable sites for hundreds of miles around, and besides, the law banning the construction of new monasteries still held. Monasteries were simply abandoned or their monks evicted by force.

In the following two years the remaining 771 monasteries were closed. Information as to how this was done is understandably hard to come by, but many indicators, such as the great number of temple ruins that are scattered about Mongolia today, suggest that not all the closures were peaceful. Some unofficial sources in Mongolia estimate that up to 50,000 monks were killed during the anti-Buddhist campaign. We will probably never know the true figures. What is clear is that the Lama Buddhist church of Outer Mongolia, which had existed for four centuries, was mercilessly harassed for a decade or so and then suddenly obliterated in just three short years. The Soviet historian Zlatkin sums it all up:

> The practice of the class struggle taught the Party that it is impossible to count on successful defence against the external enemy if the hostile organisation of traitors, saboteurs and spies in one's own rear has not been liquidated. Led by these considerations, the Party brought about the liquidation of the Lamaist counter-revolutionary centre to its conclusion in 1937 and 1938 by shutting one after the other the lamaseries implicated in hostile activity and severely punishing their heads. After this action the old feudal lamaist church in Mongolia with its numerous lamaseries, its huge herding economy, its mighty riches, its army of thousands of lamas, ceased in effect to exist.

Not surprisingly, Zlatkin's sentiments about the church echo those of most Soviet and Mongolian historians. Many

European travellers writing at the turn of the century put the blame for Mongolia's apparent feudal and backward society squarely on the shoulders of the monasteries, and this portrayal has been perpetuated in numerous texts since. A black picture has been painted of the monasteries as degenerate centres of idleness and vice. Vows of celibacy had been thrown to the wind and the temples had simply become parasites on the countryside. They sapped the rural labour force, turning economically active men into idle layabouts, and made sure the herdsmen remained poor and backward by their continual demands for favours and contributions.

This view of the Mongolian Buddhist church in the nineteenth and early twentieth centuries is reiterated in modern Western histories. Such books are full of phrases such as 'the ignorance, poverty and disease perpetuated by the unresponsive, untutored clergy', or 'the church, its dogmas, and its officers were responsible, in part, for the illiteracy, poor health, and poverty of the population'.

It was a perspective that made Bulcsu's blood boil. 'They haven't even begun to question these received prejudices. They are perpetuating this myth that Buddhism was responsible for a so-called "feudal" society,' he would begin. 'How can these guys say that the lamas were to blame for illiteracy when it was only the church that taught reading and writing? Moses [the American Mongolist, rather than his Biblical namesake] says that few of the lamas were literate since they could *only* read in Tibetan from holy books. What does he reckon they *should* have been reading?'

Bulcsu poured himself another *arkhi* and threw his empty pack of Camel cigarettes on to the table.

'Like I say, the monks were supposed to be responsible for the fact that the population had poor health, but where were the doctors trained? In the monasteries.'

He grinned. 'OK, so everyone had syphilis, but that's

not the point. I'm sure nineteenth-century London must have been rife with sexually transmitted diseases.'

He paused midway through pulling the cellophane from a new pack of Camels. He was unstoppable once he started on a tirade like this.

'Poverty. That's another thing that was supposedly the monks' fault. But how can they say that when the vast majority of the world's population lived in what we'd today call abject poverty? And as for Buddhism creaming off the profits from the land, well. I suppose the Christian church doesn't hand the plate round or own vast tracts of land that it charges rent for?'

Another Camel was pushed between his lips.

'And the notion that the monks were just sitting in their temples twiddling their thumbs is another myth. The distinction between monk and herdsman. Huh. It's a false one. Not true. There were a whole bunch of monks who lived at home and looked after their animals and only went to temples on special festivals. The country was full of these unattended temples, *sume*, which only operated on special occasions.' ·

Bulcsu lit the cigarette and took another slug of Mongolian vodka.

'All right, so there were a lot of monks who copied out Tibetan texts and translated them into Mongolian, but so what? They were economically unproductive; so are many professors, bureaucrats, artists. But it's not yet a good enough reason for killing them, is it?'

He sighed. 'They've got a lot to answer for, these Communists. Let's face it, they have to perpetuate this myth that Buddhism was degenerate because their legitimacy to rule depends upon it. And what have these great unwashed, illiterate, unhealthy people got in Buddhism's place? Most Mongolians still live in tents with no running water or sanitation, they have to queue for things in the shops, and alcoholism, a Russian disease, is a major social curse.'

More *arkhi* passed his lips.

'And there was much worse to come, of course. During the next few decades, thanks to people like Stalin, those they considered dirty, ill, ignorant or otherwise not suited to their brave new world had to be eliminated or battered into submission.'

We had spent the day at Gandan, Mongolia's last surviving operational monastery. Its full name, Gandan Tegchinlen, means 'Great Vehicle of Complete Joy', rather a misnomer in the current circumstances. It had been salutary to think, as we stood looking at the monks perched on low red benches on both sides of the approach to the altar, that this scene, once so commonplace, was now the last relic of a people's entire cultural heritage. It may have been Goering who released the safety catch from his handgun whenever he heard the word 'culture', but his actions were small fry compared to the wholesale devastation wrought by the Mongolian Communists.

We were sitting in Bulcsu's room having enjoyed a pretty standard brave new world meal of schnitzel and cucumber in the hotel dining room. On occasions like this I was an audience, unable to get a word in edgeways. The analysis was getting heavier.

'The Communists need their ideology to survive. They weren't elected, so they don't have a popular mandate. They don't have the inherited authority of emperors or kings, and they don't have the spiritual authority that comes with being an incarnate lama. Without ideology, whether it's true or false, the reason for their existence disappears.'

I wandered into the bathroom. From his position on the sofa Bulcsu forged on.

'And what is it based on?' he called. 'Well, Marx of course. But from the religious point of view the system relies on a critique of nineteenth-century European religion. It's a critique that has to be applied wherever the ideological package is used as a basis for power.'

45

I flushed the toilet.

'Basically a belief in God is simply dependent on the abstraction of certain human qualities outside the human sphere, so the theory goes. As Marx says, people who worship something which is essentially an abstraction of themselves are "alienated from themselves". These weren't actually Marx's ideas at all, they come from the minor German philosopher Feuerbach, who was nobody until Marx cottoned on to his ideas. All Marx added to the equation was that this alienation could be cured with appropriate economic measures. When economics provided "real" human happiness, it would naturally remove the need for the "false" human happiness provided by religion. The march of time would sort everything out. Once the Revolution had taken place, once Communist parties were in power, once collectivisation had been accomplished, once the means of production were in the hands of the self-appointed representatives of the people, then religion would disappear of its own accord. The fact that this train of events simply didn't happen threw the Communists into disarray. Their reaction to the obvious failure of their ideology was predictable. They couldn't admit failure, so they resorted to violence.'

'Reach for the revolver,' I chipped in.

'Well, reach for the armoured cars, the high explosives and the entire Soviet Army if necessary, more like,' Bulcsu replied. 'Of course the Mongolians never acted without good advice from Moscow, but the ultimate fate of Buddhism in Mongolia was sealed because the theory that said it would disappear was wrong, and yet it had to be proved right.'

It had been a strange day, as if we had spent it in another time zone. The monastery was a small pocket of the Middle Ages amid the harsh twentieth-century reality of

46

modern Ulan Bator. The temple atmosphere had been heady with the smells of incense and yak butter lamps and the haunting chants of the monks in their yellow silk robes and outrageous headdresses. It was a full moon and a special festival in the calendar of the Yellow Faith. The compound was full, with Mongolian senior citizens wearing their best *dels* and felt hats and polished black boots. The prayer wheels beside the temple were in constant motion, barely audible mutterings coming from the wrinkled leather faces that turned them. In front of the stupas and copper incense burners the elderly worshippers prostrated themselves on the long wooden planks.

Norbu had taken us to meet a friend of his. We had to pass through the monastery kitchens to get to his room. Great copper cauldrons bubbled with curd, and elongated barrels stood along the wall smeared with the yak's grease of a thousand meals.

The friend looked us up and down when we had been introduced. He was a small wiry man with a bald head and thick black hairs sprouting from his ears. Later, Norbu related the conversation that took place between them.

'Are they Russian?' he asked, casting a slightly nervous glance in our direction.

'No, no, they are from England,' Norbu assured him.

'England,' he said, unconvinced.

'Yes, they are Englishmen,' Norbu said.

'Englishmen,' the friend repeated. He mulled the new words over, surveying us with a thinly clad suspicion. He unwound the silk tie around his waist and pulled it tighter to give himself time to think.

'Where is England?' he asked slowly.

'It is in the west of Europe,' Norbu replied.

'Are you sure it is not in Russia?'

'Yes, yes, it is a separate country, far from Russia,' Norbu promised him.

The friend nodded. 'That is good,' he said with some

47

relief. 'Because I could not extend my hospitality to Russians.'

The four of us sat on the rough floorboards in front of a low altar. Before the small Buddhas sat a line of offerings: pieces of bread, a cup of rice, a few coins and some sweets.

Norbu's friend produced four chipped bowls and set them down in front of us. From a wooden jug he filled the bowls with what looked like a thick yellow stew. It was lumpy yak's curd that had long chunks of yak's cheese in it. We were handed the bowls. I glanced at Norbu to see how we were to eat it.

Norbu smiled. 'Wait,' he said.

His friend stepped to the altar and picked up a box of matches. Very carefully he selected two matches and put them into my outstretched hand. Everyone received a pair of matchsticks and we proceeded to eat using them like tiny chopsticks. The curd and cheese stew had a powerful, nauseous smell, but we could hardly refuse.

'Well,' said Bulcsu, 'here goes.'

We had been transported back into the Dark Ages. Monks had been eating the same stew since time immemorial, though presumably the matchsticks were a modern innovation. Otherwise, the only touchstones with the twentieth century were the metal frame of the friend's bed and the electric lightbulb dangling from the ceiling.

• ● •

All governments are guilty of double standards, but Mongolia was the first country I had seen in any detail where the contradictions of the Soviet system were quite so evident. While the Soviet Union had long championed the cause of anti-Imperialism, and had for decades been issuing venomous statements about the West's exploitation of their empires, here in Mongolia they had quietly been doing exactly the same thing for the past sixty-nine years.

All the important decisions about Mongolia's future were taken in Moscow. The presidents of the People's Republic were appointed from the Kremlin. Raw materials by the wagonload were shipped out of Mongolia to the USSR, and Mongolia had become a military camp for the Red Army, crawling with Russian troops and bristling with Soviet missiles. The Mongolian alphabet had been done away with, in favour of the more 'progressive' Russian Cyrillic, and an insidious programme was underway in schools where the youth were being taught a Russified grammar in which Russian sentence structures were taking over from Mongolian ones.

In Ulan Bator the Russian influence was plain for all to see. For Russian advisers and their families a brand of Soviet apartheid was in force. They lived in separate housing blocks with their own shops, stocked with 'riches' unavailable to the average Mongolian. These shops had guards on the door who scrutinised passes before allowing entry. The Russians also had their own bus system, always much less crowded than their Mongolian counterparts, and the wages paid to the Russian advisers were greater than those paid to Mongolians in similar positions. On several occasions people at the University had told me *sotto voce* that it was a source of friction when Russian lecturers appeared to fill jobs on double the salary that a Mongolian would be paid.

This resentment against the Russians was seldom expressed to me. When anything derogatory towards the USSR was admitted it was always out in the open where no one could overhear. It was difficult to gauge just how intense the anti-Russian feeling was, but on one memorable occasion an individual who was fairly high up in the establishment came out with a remarkable castigation.

'Lenin was a bastard. Marx was a cunt. Military socialism is supposed to last for no more than five years, but here in Mongolia we have suffered under it for sixty-five years, and the Mongolian people are very fed up.'

Yet all the time that the rape was going on the Party came out with the usual socialist ravings, although none while I was there were quite as sickly and sycophantic as one proclaimed in a book published in 1941 called *In Praise of Stalin*: 'Thanks to Stalin's concern, in the country where the Living Buddha was worshipped there appeared the industrial *combinat*; into an uncultured land there penetrated the light of culture.'

On the steps outside the Stalin State Library, where Bulcsu had struggled daily to get at the stacks of ancient Buddhist texts that he knew were piled high in an uncatalogued storehouse, there stood a fifteen-foot statue of the great man doing an impression of Lord Nelson with his hand in his tunic. In February 1990 the statue was removed after mounting public pressure. Students had crept up at night and daubed the statue with red paint to signify the river of blood that he was responsible for, and eventually the authorities had bowed to popular feeling.

One of the innovations brought about by the pressures for democracy had been a flood of new newspapers in Mongolia. Each opposition group had been allowed to publish its own news-sheets in competition with the Party's *Unen*, or *Truth*. Sainu told me that these new publications had blown the whistle on the Russians' operations in Mongolia, and that now hostility towards them was much more open. It was in the pages of these fledgling news-sheets that a debate was waged over what to do with the unwanted Stalin monument. Some suggested that it be destroyed, others that it could be re-erected somewhere in the steppe where it would not be so offensive. When it was eventually dismantled the statue was put in store, perhaps to be placed in a museum somewhere as a reminder of times past.

Statues of Stalin are not the only victims of the democratic winds of change. In the first few months of 1990 other vestiges of Soviet domination had been quietly done away with. The words of the Mongolian National Anthem were changed to remove all references to following the Soviet Union on the path to Communism, and the Mongolian alphabet was being reintroduced, to be fully taught in schools and to become official government script. President Gorbachev had already agreed to pull out all Russian troops by the end of 1992.

Religion, too, was experiencing a reawakening. It may seem strange that Gandan had been allowed to preserve the Buddhist faith at all after the ravages of the 1930s, but it did so very much under the watchful eye of the Party. It was seemingly allowed to exist for reasons of foreign policy, so that the authorities could show visiting government dignitaries what a free and open society they ran. But all the monks were Party members and many were simply conducting research into how best to overcome people's religious tendencies. Some lamas, however, had not forgotten their basic beliefs, and their voices could be heard among those clamouring for democracy. A new religious freedom was in the air in early 1990, with election candidates choosing to be photographed posing before lamas for their blessing and Gandan itself asking to be allowed autonomy from the government.

Other reminders of times past are yet to be expurgated. Although on my second visit many of the Party hoardings and posters dotted around the capital had disappeared, such as the portraits of former President Batman, which Bulcsu and I dreamt of visiting in the dead of night to paint on a caped crusader hood complete with pointy ears, others remained. On the corner opposite the main post office, V. I. Lenin still looks down reprovingly with his beady eyes at passers-by beneath the letters 'NAM', meaning Party. On a hillside on the south side of the city there remains the slogan in white stones which is updated each year. In 1990 it read: 'Long Live the 69th Anniversary of the People's Revolution'. And in the capital and in almost every settlement of any size in Mongolia one can still see hoardings depicting the legendary meeting between Lenin and the Mongolian revolutionary leader Sukhe Bator. 'Legendary' is the right word to use in this context, because although every Mongolian schoolchild is told in revered tones of this consultation with the oracle, it almost certainly never took place.

Sukhe Bator is guaranteed to remain, even in these democratic times, as a hero of the Mongolian people. After all, it was he who invited the Bolshevik army in to liberate Mongolia from the evil clutches of Baron von Ungern-Sternberg. A former dispatch-rider and typesetter and one-time soldier, Sukhe Bator, or 'Axe Hero', was one of seven members of the People's Party who travelled to Russia to seek Soviet help in 1920. The group travelled with the blessing of the Living Buddha of Urga, and his letter of authority was carried by Sukhe Bator in the handle of his riding whip, an article lovingly preserved as a relic of the Revolution in the Ulan Bator museum.

Sukhe Bator's exact role in the revolutionary process is difficult to pin down since the history of the period has been rewritten so many times. Five of the group of seven were to be liquidated on one pretext or another during the next twenty years and have become 'un-persons' in Mongolian history books. Their parts in these epic times have been variously reattributed to Sukhe Bator and the other surviving name, Choibalsan, Mongolia's version of Stalin, who was responsible for the liquidations. Perhaps one of the reasons for Sukhe Bator's guaranteed immortality is that he died young in 1923. The true circumstances of his death have also fallen victim to the censor's red pen. Some versions say that he was poisoned by enemies of the people, others that he died of an illness brought on by excessive devotion to duty.

Sukhe Bator's corpse lies in state in a mausoleum in the main square which dominates Ulan Bator: Sukhe Bator Square. The polished red granite bunker is an exact replica of the more famous tomb in Moscow's Red Square, although Mongolians never admit this. It is positioned directly in front of the main parliament building, the Great People's Hural, an awesome neoclassical structure in battleship grey.

On my first visit I walked past this monolith every day on my way to the Mongolian Institute of Hydrometeorology. Each morning I donned my thick sheepskin coat against the cold, despite the deceptive welcome of the bright blue sky, and descended the sweeping steps outside the Hotel Ulan Bator. Sitting in the middle of Sukhe Bator Square, which could have swallowed four Trafalgar Squares and still left room for more, was a larger than life statue of the great revolutionary leader himself, resplendent in red sandstone astride a charging horse. Hardly a day went by without there being a small gaggle of Soviet soldiers in their distinctive green cardboard uniforms busy taking snapshots of each other in front of the statue. If by some strange quirk of the itinerary a visitor to the capital were to miss this central monument he need not fear: Sukhe Bator's portrait still hangs in almost every public building in Mongolia.

Another aspect of the Soviet system that will take some time to disappear is the attitude of people employed in public service, which is almost everyone. There is no doubt that customers in shops or restaurants are regarded as little more than damned nuisances. The legions of waitresses at the Hotel Bayangol have perfected the art of taking absolutely no notice of people sitting at the tables awaiting service. They collect in small groups at the entrance to the kitchens, chatting or filing their nails. When forays out into the restaurant are made it is usually to straighten a tablecloth or reposition a glass as if they are expecting much more important guests at any moment. Before these forays their eyes are specially preprogrammed to avoid any contact with yours.

A polite cough or a wave of the hand is an utterly useless

way of attracting attention. A shout sometimes does the trick, but as often as not the only response it solicits is a shrug of the shoulders or an offended scowl as if to say: 'This is a restaurant, if you want to shout go into the steppe and do it.'

There are no menus to look at, but it does not matter because whatever you choose will be unavailable anyway.

Yes indeed, when the pangs of hunger have finally driven me to landing one of the waitresses in a half-nelson, she proudly announces that there is no food left. After a few more twists of the forearm the woman grudgingly admits that there may just be a schnitzel left. Since I have not had a schnitzel since breakfast I jump at the chance, and in a couple of minutes, well forty anyway, I am presented with a delectable plate of battered meat and mashed potato swimming in a congealed pool of cold gravy.

• ● •

For me, the most important change brought about by democratisation was the freedom I now had to travel outside the capital. Getting out of Ulan Bator in 1987 had been a major challenge. The restrictions on travel, both for Mongolians and foreigners, but particularly Western foreigners, were overwhelming. The basic premise was that if someone wanted to move he must be up to no good. Ordinary Mongolians that I came across were all residents of Ulan Bator and were allowed just one trip outside the capital each year, to the countryside to visit their relatives. But as Westerners, Bulcsu and I always came up against a seemingly insuperable barrier: why do you want to go? The simple reason that we were keen to see other parts of the country was not good enough. We had to have an ulterior motive and it must be a suspicious

54

one. The fact that we were not admitting it only confirmed their worst fears.

There are no public buses that run out of Ulan Bator. The only way of leaving the capital by road was by car through the militia check-points at either end of the valley, and thus permission was needed. Alternatively, travel was possible to destinations further afield by plane, but tickets had to be purchased through the state tourist agency *Zhuulchin*, and therein lay the problem.

It is not entirely accurate to say that travel for Westerners had been completely impossible. *Zhuulchin* did run trips to three destinations outside the capital, but here we came up against the total inflexibility of the bureaucracy. These trips had to be booked abroad before entering Mongolia. This we had not done.

We were in Mongolia to study, so why did we now want to travel? The idea of taking a short holiday at the end of a period of work was a total anathema to the authorities. To cap it all, we wanted to travel alone rather than in a group, which in itself was completely irregular, individual travel being a concept totally foreign to Communist travel organisations. All in all the evidence was overwhelming: everything pointed to the fact that here they had a couple of capitalist spies plotting the downfall of the Mongolian People's Republic and probably the entire Communist world into the bargain. And this in a land of nomads.

The attitude of the women behind the desks at the *Zhuulchin* offices parallelled the enthusiasm of the hotel waitresses. It took several visits before Bulcsu and I decided that a special device had been incorporated into the thick padded door which made customers entering the building invisible. Furthermore, the *Zhuulchin* staff had all been carefully selected for their task in helping the public because they were stone deaf.

I had thought that the padding on the door was protection against the bitter winter temperatures, but on further consideration it had obviously been introduced to protect the fabric from frustrated customers banging their heads against it. *Zhuulchin* was an asylum for demented travellers who wanted the impossible. If they weren't demented before they went into the building, they certainly were when they left. It was all part of the caring, fraternalistic socialist society.

It was a fitting tribute to the boredom of life in Ulan Bator that our perseverance did eventually manage to get us out of the city on a day trip. Permission had been granted from the very top, by the head of *Zhuulchin* himself, and due credit must be given to the efforts made on our behalf by Bulcsu's interpreter, the fellow named Bold.

Bold was due to pick us up at 8.30 on a Sunday morning. As we stood waiting on the steps outside the Hotel Ulan Bator, having bets as to whether he would actually appear or not, we noticed many of the passers-by were carrying shovels. A shiny black Zil pulled up outside the hotel and we jumped in. As we sped east towards the edge of town we passed many more men and women with shovels and pickaxes over their shoulders. Bold said that these people were 'Digging for Lenin', but he could not explain what exactly they were digging.

The outskirts of Ulan Bator, which continue for several miles, were a succession of *ger* compounds set back a hundred yards from the road across a patch of dust and gravel. We came to the militia roadblock and passed through on showing our papers. The guard looked at us with a mixture of puzzlement and respect. It felt good to be treated as important people who were worthy of both a vehicle and an exit pass after the long periods of humiliation suffered at the hands of the *Zhuulchin* depersonalisation team.

The city faded away and we were soon in brown country. Ulan Bator is stretched out along the valley of the River Tuul as if it has been squeezed out of a tube. The hills on either side of us looked as if they would be interesting to walk up, but Bold warned that the larch and pine forests that patch the hillsides were full of wild bears, wild goats and wild dogs, all of whom would be glad to attack and devour the casual rambler. They were particularly partial to a nice piece of Western flesh eaten on the bone, he told us with a wry smile.

Our destination was a place called Terelj, a tourist camp of rather plush *gers* and small wooden huts run by *Zhuulchin*. We were shown into one of the *gers* which was inhabited for a few days by two Russian academics from Omsk. Inside, the tent was very cosy, with carpets on the wooden floor, two beds and a couple of small sideboards. In the centre a stove was stoked with chopped logs, keeping the whole room very snug.

The academics were up and in their tracksuits and drinking vodka for breakfast. After a couple of toasts to Anglo-Soviet-Mongolian co-operation we headed off for a walk in the hills.

It was breathless work; Ulan Bator is nearly a mile above sea level and the altitude was getting to us. Bulcsu and I had to stop for regular rests to survey the scenery, but the air was of the good clean mountain variety and it felt great to be out of the city. There was a chill wind blowing but the sun was bright and our two Russian friends stripped off their tracksuit tops to reveal two very brawny chests. When we hit a bit of forest, Bulcsu and I let them forge on ahead so that they could deal with any stray bears that might fancy a take-away meal.

As we progressed through the conifers and silver birch Bold pointed out the caramel-coloured rabbit's droppings that littered the forest floor.

'These we would smoke as little children,' he said.

Not wanting to miss out on any aspect of our Mongolian experience, Bulcsu and I collected some of the pellets and on our next rest stop Bold carefully crumbled up the droppings and rolled them in a piece of newspaper. He lit the cigarette and passed it round. It tasted like rabbit's shit.

And that was the highlight of our day's outing. When we descended the hillside, having rather disappointingly not come across any savage beasts whatsoever, we downed a few more vodkas in the *ger* and amidst much backslapping climbed into the car for the return to Ulan Bator.

So it was with a faint feeling of disbelief that in the summer of 1990 I helped Sainu gather together provisions for our first venture into the proper Mongolian countryside. After many hours spent poring over maps in the temporary office behind the Young Technicians Palace, we had decided upon two separate journeys into areas that Tserendeleg thought would be interesting to take adventure tourists from Britain. Our first excursion would be to Akhangai *aimak*, a mountainous region about an hour's flight west of Ulan Bator. We would be away for a week, so it would be necessary to take food for that period.

Sainu had a Russian acquaintance who could buy the goods from one of the Russians-only stores. One afternoon we pulled up outside a building in one of the Russian suburbs of Ulan Bator. The store occupied a ground floor room in an apartment block which was painted in the customary peeling grey. As we waited in the society's black Volga, dreary Russian shoppers moved in and out of the building, some giving us sideways glances as they passed clutching their string bags of tin cans and onions. I felt like Michael Caine in one of those 1960s Cold War movies, waiting for a drop from a local agent. Sainu's friend appeared at last, a dishevelled figure who would have made the perfect undercover man. He had not shaved for several days and from the look of his clothes he had spent the time crawling round a goods yard taking notes on Soviet railway rolling stock.

We loaded the car with cardboard boxes and Sainu paid

the man off. He disappeared along a dusty street in search of his next mission.

The only thing left to buy now was some *arkhi*. Sainu had a brief parley with the driver, a youth who fancied himself with the girls in his blue denim jacket and bright red baseball cap, and he turned the key in the ignition. Nothing happened. He tried again. Still nothing. He leapt out of his seat and pulled a crank handle from the boot. Sainu took the wheel and the red baseball cap lurched down beneath the bonnet. After a couple of turns the engine spluttered into life. It was not the sort of thing that would have happened to Michael Caine.

We scoured Ulan Bator in search of drink, but to no avail. There was a national shortage of *arkhi*. I tried to bluff my way into another Russians-only store, but the stern-looking Mongolian on entrance duty was not fooled by my glum look. He closed the door in my face. Obviously there were no Russians who looked as smart and fashionable as I did, although I did not think my outfit was particularly well co-ordinated. Eventually we gave up and I had to splash out a wad of hard currency in the dollar shop. But no matter, we had everything. All was set for our first trip into the countryside.

. 4 .

THE MAN FROM OUTER SPACE

It was mid-morning when the plane touched down at Tset-serleg airport, a patch of gravel and grass that was the run-way, backed by a couple of ramshackle buildings. We taxied through the dust to a square of concrete where a huddle of people awaited our arrival. We climbed down the narrow gangway steps and joined the throng around the luggage hatch to claim our bags. As we jostled among the elbows, our guide for the next week approached and intro-duced himself. He was a middle-aged gentleman who wore a flat white cap. His grey shirt, like the ones I had loathed wearing at junior school, had several buttons missing and the fly on his khaki trousers was undone. I did not catch his name and neither did Sainu; from then on we simply referred to him as 'the gentleman'.

A second character soon joined us, a man with a cheeky grin and a brown corduroy beret. This was the driver, who eagerly grabbed our box of provisions and the heavy

Polish tent that we had brought and sprinted off through a low slung wattle and daub building into a grassless courtyard where a jeep was waiting.

It was a short drive into town along a bumpy tree-lined road of concrete slabs. We passed a series of rickety hoardings. Some had one-word Cyrillic messages on them: *Peace*, *Sport* and *Quality*. Others gave slightly more food for thought, such as *Labour is a Happy Life*, and a painting of a heavy chain breaking free from a globe with the USSR picked out in red from an otherwise green land mass. The slogan above this read *Long Live October*.

Tsetserleg was a ramshackle town. The name means 'garden', but this is little more than wishful thinking. It is the capital of the state or *aimak* known as Akhangai and consists of a few concrete buildings in the centre, the odd wooden building scattered around, and rows of *gers* in wooden palisades. We pulled up outside one of the concrete buildings, a bank where Sainu had to draw some cash from the Society's account to take on our journey. While he was inside with the gentleman I took the opportunity to stretch my legs. The sun was shining brightly and the good citizens of 'Garden City' were going about their business. The odd jeep chugged along the main street. A motorcycle and sidecar stopped at the bank and a couple wearing silk *dels* got out. I strolled across the road to where some people were gathered around a small wooden kiosk and two horses were tied to a wooden railing like the ones cowboys use to fasten their steeds to in Western films. The wooden kiosk was a shop. I peered through the crowd to see what it was selling. In the shadows behind the woman who sat reading a newspaper at the counter was an assortment of cotton shirts on a hanger. Below the hanger, set out along the floorboards of the kiosk, were some pieces of furniture painted a bright orange colour with a flowery pattern. There was a small four-legged stool, a couple of cupboards and a table with mirror attached which presumably served as a dressing table. Evidently this was the local department store.

I wandered on. At the end of the main street was a rise with a patch of tired grass and a typically Soviet-looking monstrous monument to the Revolution, a styleless concrete post with an inset of Lenin looking appropriately contemplative and beady-eyed, his goatee beard pointing downwards at the customary forty-five degree angle. Beyond the grass was an old Buddhist temple building, which, like all the temples that had been left standing after the Buddhist purges of the 1930s, was now a museum. Immediately behind the museum rose a rocky knoll. On the bare rockface were painted a number of Buddhas sitting in the lotus position, gazing straight down the main street.

When they emerged from the bank, I asked the gentleman through Sainu how long these paintings had been there. They pre-dated the Revolution apparently. They must have looked on as the Lenin monolith was erected below them, a graven image to the European 'God' who had taken over from them. But somehow the faces of the Buddhas wore just the faintest hint of a Mona Lisa-like smile, almost as if they knew that it would take more than a goatee beard to displace a faith that had been around for a few thousand years.

We sped down the main street past the Buddhas on the rockface and headed out of town. The road degraded to become a series of pot-holes with occasional stretches of concrete in between and then disappeared altogether to become a series of pot-holes in a muddy track with occasional stretches of deeper pot-holes in between. The driver stepped hard on the accelerator at the slightest hint of a vaguely flat piece of track and always left it until the very last split second before stamping on the brake and swinging the wheel to avoid a hole and puddle in the mud. The result was that Sainu and I, riding in the back of the jeep, were thrown about as if we were riding a bucking bronco. All the while the gentleman, gripping a handle fixed to the dashboard, chatted casually to the driver who was obviously in his element, brown beret sitting on the back of his head, hands tight on the steering wheel, eyes fixed to the track ahead and a look of childlike glee on his face.

Fortunately our destination was a wildlife reserve just a few miles out of town, at the entrance to a small valley, but by the time we had skidded to a halt and the driver had jumped out of his seat to unload our luggage, I felt as if I had completed a cross-country assault course.

We were taken to a *ger* and left while the gentleman and the driver disappeared to rustle up lunch. The *ger* was furnished with two beds, a knee-high table with four stools, and two wardrobes, all painted an orange flowery pattern like the furniture on sale in the wooden kiosk in town. In the centre of the *ger* stood a stove with metal chimney that poked out through a hole in the felt roof. The wooden floorboards were covered by thick geometrically-patterned carpets. This was a guest *ger*, where visiting hunters could be fed and watered before continuing further into the countryside to get down to the serious business of shooting animals.

Over lunch, a fairly standard affair of cold lamb slices with generous helpings of fat, cucumber and some slightly spicy meat chunks, the gentleman outlined our route into the Khangai Mountains. The conversation was mildly frustrating since he seldom addressed his comments to me, and Sainu had not fully donned his interpreter's hat, so that any information I gleaned was by constant questioning. We would visit two lakes to the north, a blue lake and a white lake, and a range of extinct volcanoes before returning to Tsetserleg and driving south to Genghis Khan's ancient capital at Karakorum. Although the distances were not great the roads were bad and this would take a week.

But before we could go anywhere I needed to see the museum. Mongolians are rather keen on museums. The most unlikely towns in the middle of nowhere can be guaranteed to contain a museum. They are usually well-appointed, look rather underused, and without exception are manned by a fellow with a pointer who is always very keen and proud to use it to great effect. The small white building nestling beneath the granite boulders behind the guest *ger* was the reserve's museum, and the young man in charge had been hovering around us since we arrived, pointer at the ready.

I have to admit to a certain ambivalence when it comes to museums. There is something about the way they seek to freeze things into an ordered, preserved display that makes me want to hurry through them and get out into the living world once again. Museums in Mongolia have an additional edge to them. I have the distinct impression that they are all part of an insidious Communist plot to ensure that certain aspects of Mongolia's traditional culture, such as religious articles and craftsmanship, are seen in the museum setting. By displaying such things in a museum the authorities make sure that they are associated with the past. Crystallisation in a sterile setting somehow helps to render them ineffective. Safe behind a pane of glass, they are labelled and categorised as a piece of history and thus can play no part in the present or future pattern of Mongolian life. This is the reason for the plethora of well-run and well-stocked Mongolian museums, part of the programme of education. I hope that this museum mania will undergo a review as Mongolia begins to embrace a freer society, and trades such as the ornate metalwork and decorative woodcarving become once more an accepted part of Mongolian life, rather than rejected out of hand as bourgeois activities that are incompatible with a modern scientific socialist society.

The reserve museum was what the Mongolians are pleased to call a 'natural museum'. Its exhibits were simply the wild animals and plants to be found in Akhangai *aimak*, with no controversial political or social exhibits. The young man in charge swept back the straggling locks from his eyes, straightened his fraying jacket lapels, tapped his pointer on the floor and began the guided tour.

The Khangai Mountains form the backbone of Mongolia, stretching 700 kilometres from east to west across the heart of the country. They are not particularly high for a range of Central Asian mountains, rising to just 4,021 metres at their tallest peak. The valleys are wide and flat, the grass is green in the brief summer interlude between autumn and winter, when the colour is dun before the snow falls and all is carpeted in knee-deep white. Conifers cover the hill-slopes, and the whole scene is not unlike the European Alps. Akhangai *aimak* straddles the mountain range, my guide told me, comprising seventy-six per cent pasture and seventeen per cent forest. The human population is 87,000, while livestock totals one-and-a-half million.

The Khangai is also alive with numerous species of wild animals, some of which prey on the domestic stocks of horses, yaks, sheep and goats. Wolves are the worst culprits. Some of the stuffed specimens in the wildlife museum were awesomely large: the size of small cows but more powerfully built.

The internationally endangered snow leopard also fancies the occasional domesticated dinner and is thus considered a nuisance by the herdsmen of the Khangai, who are liable to add to its endangered status with the help of their guns. When it comes to everyday practicalities, listing in the World Conservation Union's *Red Book* of threatened species counts for little. The Khangai is also home to lynx and a number of other small wild cats whose names were lost in the difficulties of translation. Badger, deer, foxes, rabbit, wild boar (jolly good meat in the autumn, the curator mentioned in passing) are all to be found. Marmots, fairly large landbound creatures that look rather like otters, are ubiquitous and stupid, the young man announced. They sit on their haunches near their holes in the steppe or on the hillside and bleat to each other. Marmots are easily mesmerised, and Mongolians hunt them using a dried white yak's tail on a stick which they wave in the air to distract the animal's attention while the hunter creeps close enough for a shot. The *aimak's* hunters had produced no less than 150,000 marmot skins last year.

Some of the Khangai's other large mammals include Argali sheep, with impressive curled horns, ibex, elk and bears. There were ten species of fish in the aquatic section of the museum, the largest of which, known as *tul* in Mongolian, was two metres long and hangs out in the region's rivers. Mongolians do not think much of fish as a meal, said my guide. When I told him that the salmon and rainbow trout in the case in front of us would be considered very good to eat in my country, he just looked at me with pity on his face.

The museum featured an interesting room of plantlife to be found in the mountains, many of which are used traditionally for medical purposes. The guide had the statistics at his fingertips when I asked for more information. 6,000 plants are used for various remedies in Mongolia, he told me, and 300 of these can be found in Akhangai *aimak*.

Our museum tour over, we were ready to roll. The driver switched on the engine and ground the jeep into gear. He looked around and smiled to see whether we were set. Sainu nodded and we leapt into motion. My small canvas bag, wedged immovably behind my seat, shot forward and thumped me hard in the back of the head. I could see this was not going to be a comfortable journey.

We left Tsetserleg behind and climbed a long dusty track out of town to the north-west, through a pass, and descended into a wooded valley with bluebells and forget-me-nots among the shadows. The wide track was chock-a-block with huge lorries struggling up and down through the trees. Some carried canvas-clad bundles of wool, others long piles of fir tree trunks, some great concrete sections of bridge. Modern commercial transport is an effort in Mongolia, where tarmac roads are almost entirely confined to city and town centres. The long-distance lorry drivers must battle along the dirt tracks, which are dry and friable during most of the summer, trailing telltale clouds of dust in their wake. Then, after a brief summer shower, the dust turns to mud and the articulated beasts slither and slide like Bambi on the ice. In winter the ground freezes solid, the ruts turn to iron and the snow obliterates the track. Like many of the animals in this country of extremes, the lorries are put to bed and hibernate until the great spring thaw when the landscape is once more amenable to modern transport.

A couple of hours out of Tsetserleg we stopped at a huge granite boulder in a wide flat green valley. The rock, known as 'Taikhar Chuluu', stood a good ten metres high and as many across and was covered in graffiti. Legend has it that the rock was put down here by a large wrestler who had been called in by the local herdsmen to deal with a problematic serpent which was alienating itself from the local community by eating their livestock. The wrestler grappled with the serpent and after an epic fight delivered the *coup de grâce* by squashing it beneath the boulder. The hero is commemorated by a large statue in the central park in Tsetserleg.

The landscape was wide and green. Every so often we drove past a *ger* or two alone in the verdant expanse. A herd of sheep would dash *en masse* to avoid us, horses and yaks would look up from their quiet grazing as we sped past. Wisps of smoke rose from the vertical metal chimneys of the *gers*. A horseman would give us a studied look, no wave, just a gaze. Occasionally the stream that ran through the valley would meander and anastomose and feed a line of willows in the otherwise treeless grasslands. Everywhere marmots would sprint away across our track and disappear into their holes.

The valley became boggy and the lush grass coloured by great swathes of yellow buttercups, orange flowers and blue irises. The jeep became a bronco once again and bucked its way through the axle-deep mud, its four-wheel drive screaming. An unseen cuckoo called to us from the hilltops. The valley was narrowing and we pulled up at the river. The gentleman and the driver got out. They did not look happy.

'The river is too high,' the gentleman announced, 'we must cross it three times to reach the blue lake, but it is too high.' He pulled off his white cap and scratched his head.

The driver had dashed off up the bank to see whether there was an easier place to traverse the fast-flowing water that was perhaps three feet deep over round granite pebbles. He returned and pulled a pair of thigh-length waders from behind his seat.

'It has snowed last night,' the gentleman explained, 'so the water is deep.' The driver was scrambling over the cobbles, a long stick in hand, testing the depth. He turned and smiled, knee-deep in the babbling waters, and shrugged his shoulders.

I cajoled, encouraged and bullied, explaining that I had come all the way from England and that it would be very disappointing to be beaten by a small river. Could we not wait until later in the day when the mountain waters began to freeze again and the flow was stemmed? The Mongolians were not impressed with my pleas, but it was decided to stop and 'have a snack', as Sainu put it. We collected some wood for a fire.

Mongolians have very healthy appetites and since their idea of a proper meal consists of large quantities of meat and little else, the loaf of bread and tins of preserved food that were produced were considered simply a hole-filler until we could find some real food. From the box of provisions Sainu had obtained from the Russian shop in Ulan Bator he selected a glass jar of pickled vegetables, a tin of goulash and another of 'chicken in juice', which would have been more accurately labelled 'bones in juice with a few scraps of meat if you're lucky'. The driver had his own supply of Mongolian liver paté which for some reason was labelled in both Cyrillic and English, although the English version declared the contents to be 'liver pastry'. These delights, spread on large hunks of bread, were to become our staple snacks of the trip.

The driver prepared the tea, which, in the absence of milk, was made Russian style. The water was salted and brought to the boil and then the tea sprinkled into the bowl and left to stew for a while. The first ladleful was thrown to the winds, 'for Khangai and the gods'.

After we had eaten, the driver carefully 'broke' the fire by moving away one of the three stones on which the tea bowl had stood. Fire is traditionally considered to be very powerful by Mongolians, and this breaking of the fire is always done because, having made the fire do your work, you should never leave it imprisoned.

The snack seemed to do the trick. Once we had cleared the eating things away the driver and the gentleman went into a short parley while surveying the river and decided that it was worth a try. We jumped into the jeep, the driver backed it up, and put his foot down. With much swinging of the wheel, splashing of water and a few ominous judders when a wheel made contact with the larger rocks, we made it to the opposite bank, much to everyone's relief. The peril of the situation was brought home two days later on our return, when at exactly the spot we had just managed to cross, we came upon a small truck marooned in midstream. It had got stuck later the same day. We came across the driver at a *ger* some miles beyond, still waiting for the river to fall enough to get his vehicle out.

The light was beginning to fade as we continued up the

valley towards the blue lake. After the first river crossing the next two were relatively straightforward affairs, although each time the thought went through my mind that we could be in trouble should more snow fall while we were above the river and it were to swell even more by the time we wanted to come back this way.

At 10.30 we stopped near the river by a small clump of Siberian pines and had some fun putting up the two-man tents by the light of the moon. We got a fire going and drank bowls of salty tea by the crackling flames.

Once the sun had gone the air was crisp and cold; there were thick wedges of unmelted snow by the young conifers on the river bank.

• ● •

Several times during the night I was woken by what seemed to be a block of ice growing in the small of my back, each time to pull on another shirt or a jumper. At sun-up I emerged into the dewy dawn wearing every stitch of clothing I had brought with me, to be met face to face with a shaggy grey wolf. We stood looking at each other for a few seconds, neither quite sure who was the more surprised. I dived back into the tent to grab my spectacles, but when I reappeared with an enhanced viewing capacity the beast was gone.

After a breakfast of liver pastry, another tin of goulash, and tea, we were off once more. The track had all but disappeared and the going was bumpier than ever, the terrain littered with boulders in the grassy carpet. Soon the springy turf gave way to bog and the driver, who had wrestled valiantly until now, declared that it was impossible to continue, so we took to our feet.

The sun beat down as we marched through the conifers, the marshy ground awash with wild flowers, including several types of orchid and chives to chew on. The gentle-man removed his shoes and left them on a fallen tree to be picked up on our return. We crossed several babbling brooks on their way down to join the main river before we emerged above the treeline on to a moorland terrain with breathtaking views down the valley we had climbed the previous day. Away down the hillside a herd of yaks was moving out to its morning pasture. There was not a sound to be heard save for the rustling of the breeze in the bog grasses and another cuckoo, as usual out of sight but loudly commentating on our progress.

Rather breathless at our high altitude march, we came eventually upon the blue lake, a wide expanse of crystal water largely covered by a permanent layer of ice. Its prox-imity had been indicated by a large *oboo*, or monument to the gods of the lake, built with long wooden sticks stood on their ends like a North American wigwam. Inside the structure, which was taller than a person, were various offerings: coins and sweets, matches and matchboxes and one or two empty *arkhi* bottles. With the sun high in the sky, we all lay down like animals on the cobbles at the water's edge and drank long draughts of the cold lake water.

The two-hour climb to the blue lake became a forty-minute canter down again to where the jeep was standing. A little further down the valley, before crossing the river, we pulled up at a couple of *gers*. The gentleman looked around for signs of a dog and gingerly climbed out of the vehicle. The dogs stationed outside country *gers* are half-wild and vicious. Any stranger approaching their people's *ger* is considered fair game, and if you are set upon by one of these animals there is little hope unless the owner appears to call it off. I have read in a nineteenth-century traveller's account of a journey in Mongolia that one self-preserving ploy that sometimes works is to squat down as if you are relieving yourself, since often all these dogs get to eat is human excrement.

None of us felt ready to put this theory to the test, however, so we stayed in the jeep and let the gentleman run the gauntlet. He approached the patterned wooden door of the *ger*, buttoned his jacket, pulled down his cuffs and sleeves, and disappeared inside. A few minutes later he poked his head out and beckoned us to join him.

Inside, the *ger* was dark and full of shadows, the only light coming from the semicircle in the roof from which the felt had been pulled back. Our host sat squatting on the floor to the right of the central stove. He wore a dirty *del* and large black riding boots; his face was shiny and weatherbeaten from a life herding animals. He grinned to reveal several missing front teeth as I greeted him with, '*Sain Bainu*'. I was directed to a small wooden stool at the back of the *ger* and to the left, positioned next to the gentleman. Sainu and the driver sat themselves down on the metal-framed bed next to me. On the other side of the *ger* was a second bed. Slowly my eyes grew accustomed to the dark. The rough wooden floorboards were covered with animal skins – a yak and a couple of goat hides. Behind me was a small dressing table, the glass a patchwork of black and white snapshots of what I assumed to be friends and relatives, and some religious paintings. All around the cloth-covered walls of the tent hung strings threaded with small hard blocks of yak's curd and cheese. Around the door where we had just entered was a collection of large metal and wooden bowls and a bulging leather bag made from two goat skins sewn together. A wooden ladle poked out from the neck. Sainu's eyes lit up when he saw the bag and he pointed to it to explain that this was full of *airag*, a Mongolian summer delicacy, fermented mare's milk. But we were unlucky, the *airag* was not ready for drinking. Another drink was produced instead, in a very old glass bottle. This was real *arkhi*, the gentleman told me, distilled from yak's milk here in the *ger*.

A thimble of a cup began to go the rounds. Each time

the host would fill and pass it to one of us. The gentleman was first. The cup was handed over with the outstretched right arm touched or held at the elbow with the left hand. Once the liquid was consumed, the cup was passed back to the host to refill and hand on to the next in line. The yak's *arkhi* was clear and greasy with small bits floating in it, apparently a sign of good quality. It was potent stuff.

The man's wife appeared through the door, followed by four children. The kids were between five and seven years old, three girls and a boy. The woman piled a plate high with milk products, a crumbly yellow cheese, a hard boiled white curd, some pieces of flat white squidgy stuff that was some form of clotted cream and some hard white sugar lumps.

It was a strange scene, tucked inside this *ger* in the middle of the Mongolian mountains, eating and drinking the products of the countryside. We were plied with more *arkhi* and food, but there was little conversation. The host seemed relaxed and not at all interested.

The children, however, took up position on the skins around their dad and gazed at me with fixed stares. I smiled at them but got no reaction. They just stared with furrowed brows and large brown eyes, as if they were looking at someone who had arrived from another planet. I tried poking my tongue out at them and puffing my cheeks, actions silly enough to get a smile out of the most recalcitrant child in England. But the Mongolian kids' stares remained, unmoved at the strange facial expressions of the man from outer space.

My Mongolian friends obviously felt at home. The driver picked a screwed-up ball of newspaper from the sideboard, tore off a strip and proceed to roll himself a cigarette from the tobacco inside. Sainu was busy tucking into the blocks of curd plastered with the clotted cream and topped with a sugar lump. The gentleman was now chatting to the host every now and again, and produced his snuff bottle wrapped in a silk pouch. Snuff is very popular in Mongolia, its exchange another gesture of friendship between passing strangers. Like the *arkhi*, there is a proper way to offer the bottle. The gentleman took a snort, pushed the pink coral stopper with attached spoon half-way back into the top of the bottle and handed it over to the host with the right hand again touched at the elbow with the left. The small bottle is held vertically in an open palm, resting on the little finger and taken with the outstretched fingers of the receiver in a scraping-like motion, the tips of the fingers brushing as the bottle is taken.

After the rounds of the snuff, which reduced me to sneezes, much to the amusement of all around, the driver stood up and left the *ger*. Since no one seemed to take any notice and no offence was taken, I followed him. He had unleashed the horse from its tether on a goalpost and was cantering around. There was a refreshing lack of the Western embarrassment I would have had at doing such a thing. I could not imagine walking into a cottage in the English countryside, eating and drinking my fill and then abruptly walking out to have a drive in the farmer's tractor.

Sainu poked his head out of the *ger* to warn me of the dog, but I had been followed by the children, for whom I continued to be a source of total amazement. I took my cameras from the jeep, and every window was immediately manned by a small face gazing in wonderment at me and the contents of the vehicle. Pointing my camera at the children, however, got an instant response. They scattered in all directions, re-forming at distance, hands to their faces. I returned to the jeep, took a tin of boiled sweets and made sure they all saw me pop one into my mouth. I offered the tin with outstretched arm. The small boy approached first, his eyes fixed on the coloured square slabs in the tin. The girls followed suit and all stood sucking, eyes on me waiting for my next move. I raised my camera once more, and the children did not run. I had won them over. For the two younger girls the procedure was still baffling, but the boy and elder girl knew what was going on and stood bolt upright, hands straight down by their sides, chests out, with very serious looks on their faces. They thought the whole process was fun and wanted me to take some shots of them cutting wood. This involved the two younger girls sitting on one end of a log like a rocking horse to steady it, while the other two took each end of a long saw.

A second boy appeared on his horse with the yaks we had seen up the valley earlier in the day. I have not come across a better description of this shaggy mammal, known as a *sarlick* in Mongolian, than that written by one of Baron von Ungern-Sternberg's sidekicks, Dmitri Alioshin:

> The *sarlick* is a peculiar animal, to say the least, and I never could get used to it. It resembles the cow, buffalo, horse, poodle, boar and rhinoceros.

Alioshin also saw another aspect of the yak's character that I never had confirmed to me:

> Of its own accord it will attack and chase wolves and kill them. It likes raw meat, and has a great appetite for dead men, whom Mongols usually throw out of their *yurts*.

It was round-up time and all the children were dispatched to bring in the goats. Apparently we were staying for dinner, and as the goats neared the wooden pen one of the little girls was sent into the pack. She grabbed a goat and sat on it while her brothers and sisters pulled the bleating animal to their father who was waiting in front of the *ger* with a knife at the ready.

Daddy pushed the goat on to its back and two of the children held its legs as the knife went into its chest just below the ribs, a short cut. The man plunged his hand into the animal's chest and pulled out a handful of white mess. The goat looked up from its unceremonious position with a puzzled frown on its face like a soon-to-be-retired schoolmaster whose class has got out of control. The animal was bleating continuously, as if it was asking, 'Hey, what's going on here?' The family team held it in position and it took about twenty seconds to die.

The skinning and disembowelling was a very efficient process. Quick cuts were made down the inside of each leg and along the goat's belly from neck to tail. The hide was removed by tugging at the skin with one hand while ramming the clenched fist of the other between skin and flesh. Once peeled, the carcass lay on a carpet of its own making. Only the hoofs were cut off and discarded, otherwise all parts of the unfortunate beast were kept. The first dissection was to remove the entrails, heart and lungs, which released a small pool of thick red blood that lay neatly inside the carcass and was poured off into a bowl. Throughout the butchery not a drop of blood was spilled; apparently, if the animal is killed by squeezing the heart like this the whole system simply stops abruptly and there will be no bleeding. The meat of animals killed in this way is more gamey than meat which is drained of its blood. As the animal was cut up and the meat placed in a large bowl to be boiled, the wife flushed out the intestines with water brought from the river. We were to eat outside, and a stove was produced for the purpose.

While the meat was boiling the mother took me inside, sat me down with a bowl of Mongolian tea and proceeded to show me the method for distilling yak's *arkhi*. A large metal bowl was placed on the topless stove and filled with fermented curd from a wooden urn. As the curd came to the boil a hollow metal tube the size of a barrel was carefully placed on top of the bowl and the join sealed with a strip of rag. On top of the tube a second bowl was placed, this one filled with cold river water so that the alcohol would condense on its underside.

This was proper *arkhi* that I was watching being made.

The wheat spirit bought in bottles in all the towns is vodka which was introduced by the Russians, but this was the home-distilled country stuff which had been drunk long before the Soviets had introduced vodka *arkhi*. It was illegal, apparently, to distil your own, although I never really hit on an adequate explanation of why. I suppose it is a combination of trying to suppress a traditional cottage industry and at the same time protection of the monopoly of the state distillers that produce the vodka.

When dinner was ready we all sat cross-legged around the stove on the grass behind the *ger*. The two little girls produced the yak's hide for the visitor from outer space to sit on. We started with bowls of goat soup, drunk piping hot with much slurping. Then a small piece of meat was thrown into the stove for the gods, and the real eating began. Large chunks of meat, each the size of a Sunday family joint at home, were handed out and we all tucked in with our knives, cutting hunks from the joint and gobbling them off the blade. Some very mutilated wild onions were produced for me, to add a vegetable dimension to my meat.

My second joint was the breastbone, the prize piece, which I had to slice up and pass around to all before I could start on it myself. The kids were not part of the feast, they hovered around the edge of our semicircle and grabbed any scraps they could. By now their numbers had been swelled by an older girl and a boy who had just returned from school, a *ger* up the valley. This made seven in total.

The *arkhi* had started to loosen everyone's tongues and our host, whose name was Batsagaan, began to tell me about himself and his family. He had eighty-five livestock, he proudly informed me, although presumably that number was now eighty-four as we were chewing the boiled goat. He was a good hunter and had won several *aimak* prizes. His favourites were wild boar, which he tracked in the forests in autumn. Boar was good meat, with as much as twenty centimetres of fat around the body of a large animal as winter approached.

Batsagaan had lived in this valley all his life, moving with the seasons between green pastures and winter stables where his yak, goats, sheep and horses were fed on hay. He complimented me on my healthy appetite for meat, telling me, as he passed one of the goat's hind legs, that I must be a Mongolian at heart.

The conversation turned to politics. Batsagaan thought the forthcoming democratic elections were very important. He would vote for the old Party, he said. This was not surprising, as it turned out, since when the government jeep arrived at his *ger* with his ballot paper it would have the name of just one candidate on it. But this did not perturb Batsagaan. The candidate had been nominated by the people of the area and he was a good man.

Herders like Batsagaan are the backbone of support for the Communist Party, or the Mongolian People's Revolutionary Party, to give it its official title. No one was in any real doubt as to the outcome of the first multi-party democratic elections in the country's history, since herders and their families make up more than half of Mongolia's population, and a lack of candidates in the countryside was a problem that hampered all the opposition parties. There was also a general suspicion of the largely urban-based opposition groups.

'They do not understand our life in the countryside,' Batsagaan explained. It was a complaint I was to hear many times. Members of the Democratic Party, who had been the major instigators of the democratic movement in Mongolia, had baffled the country people with some of their political tactics. In March, Democratic Party leaders, frustrated at the government's slow response to their demands for moves towards democracy, had staged a hunger strike in Ulan Bator. While hunger strikes may be a recognised, if extreme, form of political action in the

Western world, in Mongolia such a protest was unheard of. Country people particularly were bewildered.

'We have a good life,' said Batsagaan, 'but feeding seven children is not easy. Why did the politicians refuse to eat any food?' he asked incredulously.

The old Party would continue to look after the affairs of the country folk, Batsagaan explained. It was the government, until that time synonymous with the Party, who had encouraged them to build the winter barns and feed lots for the herders' livestock. Batsagaan contributed milk products, meat and wool to the *aimak* government and used any of the remainder for himself. The government also now allowed him to sell his animals or produce in the nearest town if he needed cash for clothes or tools. But the Batsagaan family were pretty self-sufficient in their valley in the Khangai. They cut trees for fuel, they ate from the products of their herd, many of their household implements Batsagaan had made himself, including a brand new wooden cart complete with wooden wheels, that he proudly showed me. The hue of the government in Ulan Bator apparently made little difference to his life. It made no odds whether or not he could get a passport and travel to other countries, for example. He was a Mongolian, had never left his beloved valley in the Khangai, and had no desire to do so. He probably did not even know what a passport was.

By the end of the evening my stomach was as tight as a drum, I had eaten so much goat. It was just as well we were all lying stretched out on the grass because the gentleman would certainly have fallen off a stool, he had drunk so much yak's *arkhi*. He impressed upon me how lucky I was to have seen the blue lake, somewhere all Mongolians knew of but few had been fortunate enough to visit. Only a few years before, the President himself had made the trip. Any visitor to the blue lake will enjoy three years of good health and good fortune, Batsagaan chipped in. I guessed the President must have made a wrong move during his lakeside visit since he had been forced to resign in March.

We were all in high spirits as we pulled away in the jeep after a drawn-out handshaking session which, for the kids, was my final bizarre act. The gentleman led the way with some drunken songs about rivers and horses and women with long hair as we bounced away down the valley. I do not remember how we put up the tents that night.

. 5 .

WHITE LAKE, BLACK FLIES

There was a rather subdued air to our party the next morning, but my companions soon brightened up when the tea was brewing and the driver produced some choice pieces of cold boiled goat wrapped in a newspaper. Real food for breakfast. I managed a few chunks from the bone, but when the others began to fill their bowls of tea with the congealed meat I have to admit I declined to further my Mongolian repast.

Loading the jeep I took charge of personally. I was fed up with pieces of luggage or equipment shooting over the back of the seat every time we encountered a bump. When I was finally content that no item could possibly be dislodged from the intricate arrangement of weight, size and shape, we set off. Pulling away from the river bank, I was just entering that pleasant feeling of semi-slumber after a hard night when I was rudely brought back to reality by a very solid whack to the side of my head from one of the legs of goat that hung suspended from the jeep ceiling. The animal had been dead for twelve hours, but was still kicking; it was obviously getting its own back.

There was a full day's driving ahead of us, along the Khangai range to a nature reserve encompassing some extinct volcanoes and another lake: the white lake. Akhangai is one of Mongolia's smallest *aimaks*. It covers about 55,000 square kilometres, or nearly three times the size of Wales. We were soon travelling along its main highway, as wide as a motorway but without the tarmac. We passed a large number of cultivated fields, some with antiquated Soviet machinery chugging along between the furrows.

'What are they growing in those fields?' I asked Sainu.

'Growing,' he said, and there was a long pause. Then finally, 'Make of flour.'

'Wheat?' I asked.

'Make of flour, yes.'

Mongolia has had some notable achievements in the field of agriculture since the Revolution, according to that informative little publication *Mongolia and the Soviet Union: Sixty-five Years of Friendship and Co-operation*. As recently as 1957 the country grew no grain whatsoever, but just ten years later Mongolia not only produced its entire domestic needs for this basic foodstuff, but also had enough left over to export to the outside world. Like many of the facts the booklet contains, the first part of this statement is not entirely true. Although Mongolians have long been a nomadic people, and thus much more interested in tending their livestock than ploughing fields, the cultivation of grain and other crops has in fact been practiced on a small scale for at least a hundred years, although traditionally Mongolians obtained most of their grain by trade with settled neighbours.

Like so many developments in the Mongolian economy, the drive to become self-sufficient in grain was a copycat exercise taken from the Soviet Union. At the same time that Khrushchev set his 'Virgin Lands' scheme into motion in western Siberia and Kazakhstan in the late 1950s, so the Mongolians began to put their steppes to the plough. By so doing, the Soviets initiated one of the greatest ecological disasters in their history; the Mongolians did the same. Just as, thirty years before, the sod-busting pioneers of the American Great Plains found to their cost that semi-arid grasslands do not take kindly to mechanised farming techniques, the central planning authorities of the Communists stumbled upon the same result: the whole lot blew away in a cloud of dust.

'Mistake' was a word traditionally reserved by Communists for use only when talking about Western ways of doing things, so I was interested to hear Sainu's view on the subject now that things were more open. Needless to say, he had never heard of the disaster. It was just another skeleton in the Communist cupboard that would no doubt have its bones rattled at some point in the future.

The long, thin cultivated fields we were now passing, a response to the dusty disaster of the 1960s that offers some protection to the soil by the intervening strips of grass, are largely run by state farms. The Mongolian dustbowl notwithstanding, these state farms have been pretty successful in their declared aim of feeding the nation with bread, even if this aim was all part of a more insidious scheme to settle and thereby control a population that was traditionally always on the move. Collectivisation, the other agricultural ruse adopted from the Soviet Union, has had a more troublesome history.

The collectivisation of animal herding was started in 1929 as an action replay of what was happening in Stalin's Russia. It was just as brutal and repressive, but even less successful, since Mongolia was simply not ready for such a move. The notion that Mongolia was ticking over on the ideological runway ready for take-off into a complete realisation of socialism was completely unfounded. The country lacked all the ground support staff and back-up in the form of trained managers, technicians or teachers, and its pilots, the Party's Central Committee, had only a vague idea of where the destination was and little knowledge of how to fly a plane. To cap it all, the passengers, the herdsmen of the steppes, were simply not interested in making the journey. The end result was that animal herding, the mainstay of the country's economy, was assiduously ruined. This period of the early 1930s was a time that the Party were pleased to call the 'Great Leap Forward'.

An account of the operation in Akhangai *aimak* details how the whole process of confiscation of livestock from wealthier individuals and monasteries and its distribution as common property to collectives which first had to be set up, took just twenty days.

> We arranged meetings with the local poor and middle herdsmen, and we explained the decrees of the Party and the government to them, elicited their criticisms about the way the nobles whose property had just been confiscated had oppressed the masses during the time of the despotic government, and then explained to them that people's communes would be established and the confiscated property transferred to them as common property.

> The team carrying out the job were met with a complete lack of enthusiasm. The only people remotely interested were a bunch of crippled and blind beggars who had formerly 'aunted the lamaseries. They thought a commune sounded like a place where they might get a bite to eat. Otherwise, no one was keen to look after the new animals which were regarded as stolen property, and the new leaders of the communes had no idea of what they were supposed to be doing. While the Central Committee in Ulan Bator could hail the founding of some 400 collectives throughout the country in just two years as a great victory for socialism, in reality the boast meant little more than a collapse of herding, the country's main source of

wealth. By 1932 socialism's victory had cost Mongolia seven million beasts, or roughly one-third of the national herd. The 'Great Leap Forward' had turned into a crippled backward somersault.

Partly as a result of this blind rush towards the socialist panacea of collectivisation and partly due to the concomitant move against the Buddhist establishment, Mongolia was reduced to civil war in the early 1930s. It took a visit from the Red Army and a directive from the Comintern in Moscow to change things, confirming a power structure that was to continue until the late 1980s. While the Party leaders reformed and pursued a more calculated approach to the religion 'problem' later in the decade, the collectivisation fiasco was abandoned. The so-called 'New Turn' that followed in the second half of the 1930s saw a complete about-face with regard to agriculture. All the collectives were dismantled and private herds were encouraged in a desperate attempt to save the country from disaster.

It was not until the mid-1950s that collectivisation was once more declared Party policy, since it was 'an essential prerequisite to the building of socialism in the country', as the then President, Tsendenbal, put it. This time the process took slightly longer than twenty days. Indeed, the programme had been ten years in the planning and was that much better organised. But collectivisation was still not exactly a response to popular demand, and a barrage of propaganda and economic incentives was needed to get the job done. Economic incentives took the form of allotting pastures for the exclusive use of collectives, so reducing the grazing available to individual herders, and placing much heftier tax demands, in the form of produce, on private operators. Although to begin with herders were allowed to keep a certain number of livestock for their private use, this number was drastically cut soon after. Then the wages paid to individuals from the collectives' funds were increasingly paid in cash rather than in kind, and it was not long before the herders had been successfully transformed from self-sufficient individuals into wage-earning workers. The whole process was as much an exercise in social engineering as a transformation in farming methods. The Party had achieved the desired result: the country's herders had become the proletariat, a group without which Communism had little meaning.

It is a tribute to the maniacal fervour of the men in charge of Mongolia's development, in Moscow as much as in Ulan Bator, that the achievement of the socialist aim was so important to them that it could even be pursued in a country that had no proletariat at the time of the Revolution. This is one of the extraordinary aspects of the progress of Communism in this Central Asian state. When the Revolution came in 1921, Mongolia had few if any of the symptoms of a society ready for development along Marxist lines. 'It was the antithesis of the industrial society in which the proletariat would be the vanguard of the revolution,' comments one Western historian of the country's affairs. Whereas on paper Marxist development should be ignited by a working class revolt, Mongolia bucked the system by not having a working class to do the revolting. Hence the masterminds in Moscow had apparently reasoned: 'Let's have a Revolution there and then set about creating a working class who can inherit the Communist panacea.'

Almost as remarkable is the fact that all this jiggery-pokery was carried on behind closed doors. For decades this country the size of western Europe had been sealed off from the outside world and subjected to a nationwide ideological experiment. The Mongolian people, in their reassessment of their country's situation, will certainly have a lot of material to keep the historians occupied for some time to come.

• ● •

Black clouds were collecting overhead when we eventually arrived at the entrance to the Horgo nature reserve at around five in the afternoon. There was a small town near the entrance, a motley collection of wooden shacks and *ger* compounds which looked appropriately stark and frontier-like against the backdrop of craggy volcanic peaks and angry skies. We pulled up at a red and white barrier across the track and the driver disappeared inside a small hut beside it.

The reserve was popular with hunters and Mongolian tourists, Sainu explained to me while we waited; it received 4,000 visitors each year. As if to confirm the statement, a small bus rounded the hillside in front of us and lurched along the track towards us. It stopped on the other side of the barrier and its driver climbed out. The bus was full of children on holiday from Ulan Bator. Their trip had been organised by the city's department store, The Big Shop.

We drove into the reserve, winding our way between the hills, and stopped. The gentleman explained that I ought to see the volcano. We climbed a steep path up a hillside strewn with pumice and other volcanic rubble. The pieces of black rock were pockmarked all over like sponges, but sharp and extremely hard underfoot. The place had an eerie quality to it as the dark clouds scudded across the sky, throwing occasional shafts of bright sunlight on to the innumerable tall piles of stones erected to the gods of the volcano. These *oboos* marched across the hillside in all directions as far as the eye could see. Some sported sticks in their centres with ragged pieces of cloth attached, flapping in the wind. The odd tuft of grass clung to the jagged slopes, and wild flowers were dotted over them as if splashes of orange, yellow, white and purple paint had been spattered across the lunar landscape.

We reached the summit and stood among the stone monuments that were perched on the rim, peering vertically down into a perfect cone. Its insides were smoothed ·

by fans of stones and rocks. Large raindrops were now hitting our faces, driven by the wind which tore at our shirtsleeves and trousers. The driver and the gentleman placed rocks on the *oboos* and agreed that there were powerful gods in this place.

In front of us stretched the reserve. The white lake, on whose shores we would pass the night, wound its way behind a distant peak. Below us several other craters had been blistered out of the earth and from them wide tongues of lava spread out over the plains. Here and there fluorescent green pine trees had grasped a root hold, like vanguards of nature attempting to quell the ancient wasteland. But they had some way to go yet. Horgo had a haunted atmosphere, as if this was primaeval earth in residence, and no place for nature or people.

It was another hour's drive to the lakeside, along a winding track which made all the other Mongolian tracks seem as smooth as snooker tables. The jeep bucked its way along at five miles per hour, hurling us and all its contents in every direction. The clouds descended and enveloped us in a swirling mist, rain splattered against the windscreen and the wind screeched, but when we emerged at the smooth lake shore the storm had subsided. High above, scrappy clouds still raced across the sky, but over the lake there was a strange calm. A mist hung above the glassy water, and along the shore a line of *oboos* stood shiny and black.

We jumped out of the vehicle and into a cloud of flies. They were large and black and biting. The driver handed out Russian cigarettes and we all started smoking furiously in an attempt to fend off the airborne attack.

'Do English tourists like flies?' Sainu asked. I thought they would not, as I hastily rubbed my stick of insect repellent over every piece of exposed flesh. 'Then this is a problem, yes?' he suggested helpfully. It was, since Bayer Chemicals Limited of Germany had obviously never come across this particular species of aerial persecutor.

But the flies were not our only difficulty. There was not a tree in sight and therefore no wood for a fire. We took off again across the grass towards a wooden shelter nestled below the hillslopes. It was a winter corral and we managed to unearth some damp dung and the odd stick of wood. To help get the fire started, the weather provided some fine drizzle and we had to resort to a splash of petrol. Then out came the goat and we settled down to eat.

'There are many salmon fishes in this lake,' Sainu told me, 'very easy to catch. A fish will jump every time we throw out the line.' It was unfortunate we had no fishing rod; salmon would have been a welcome change from the goat. But remembering the look of disdain on the face of the museum guide when I mentioned eating fish, I wondered if Sainu and company would eat it if we had been able to catch any. 'Mongolians can eat if it is necessary,' replied Sainu, 'but meat is much better.' Contrary to popular belief, some early records indicate that Mongolians have in times past enjoyed a bit of fish in their diet. But fishing probably ceased with the introduction of Buddhism, since water animals and fish are one of the lowest forms of reincarnation and it was not the done thing to sit down to a dinner of such ignoble creatures.

The white lake certainly seemed like a good spot to bring my adventure tourists. The surrounding hills were good places to collect berries and walnuts and see the wildlife, the scenery was spectacular and the fishing apparently good. We spent the following day wandering around the lake, without the flies which had mysteriously disappeared. A few gulls circled over the lake and a distant cuckoo punctuated the tranquil silence.

We hit the trail late that afternoon, bound for Tsetserleg. After an hour we stopped at the 'tree with a hundred branches', an important Shamanic tree apparently whose branches were tied with coloured ribbons. Our journey was also frequently interrupted by stops at various *gers* along the way. At the second stop the gentleman, who was always first to brave the possibility of being savaged by the dogs, emerged from the tent holding a china bowl, his face beaming. Here, at last, the *airag* was ready for drinking.

We all piled into the *ger* and took up our customary positions at the back and to the left as we entered. A round-faced man with a pork pie hat pulled down tight on his head was squatting by the stove in the centre of the tent pouring the fermented mare's milk into bowls from a white plastic gear oil can. The liquid had a thin consistency, more watery than cow's milk, and floating on its surface were small greasy globules and the odd horse hair for authenticity. It did not taste of anything much, a bit like drinking cold washing-up water, I thought, but the boys were in their seventh heaven and poured bowl after bowl of the stuff down their throats.

Mongolians will drink twenty litres of *airag* or more every day during the summer, and as much as forty litres if they are particularly thirsty. It is an ancient drink, enjoyed in Genghis Khan's times and widely used in traditional ceremonies of all kinds, both to drink and to sprinkle on the ground. Being a product of the horse, supreme animal of the nomads, and white into the bargain, the colour of goodness, purity, richness and peace, a splash of *airag* was always good policy before worship of any kind, whether Shamanic or Buddhist.

The technique for collecting the milk and making *airag* is the same today as it was 700 years ago. A detailed account of the process, made by the medieval traveller William of Rubruck, still holds good in the late twentieth century.

They stretch along the ground a long rope attached to two stakes stuck in the earth; and at about nine o'clock they tie to this rope the foals of the mares they want to milk. Then the mothers stand near their foals and let themselves be peacefully milked.

And so, when they have collected a great quantity of milk, which is as sweet as cow's milk when it is fresh, they pour it into a large skin or bag and they begin churning it with a specially made stick which is as big as a man's head at its lower end and hollowed out; and when they beat it quickly it begins to bubble like new wine and to turn sour and ferment, and they churn it until they can extract the butter. Then they taste it and when it is fairly pungent they drink it.

Sainu was very happy. He wiped his mouth with the back of his hand after his third bowlful and handed the vessel to the pork pie hat man for a refill. He patted his stomach and smiled. 'Good *airag*,' he declared. The gentleman was noisily slurping on his stool beside me, and the pork pie hat handed the gear oil can to his wife who had just appeared to refill it by ladle from the bulging goat skin hanging next to the door. It was the first of the season, and the boys were going to drink as much as they could.

'*Airag* is very good for digestion,' said Sainu. 'It has all the vitamins needed by the body, therefore very health-giving. It is very good with meat.'

It is also very proficient at flushing out the system, as I found later to my cost, and is therefore used sometimes as a medicine.

By the time we had reached Tsetserleg late that night, we had stopped another four times for *airag*, and at the last tent the driver had rinsed out one of his jerrycans and filled it with the fermented milk for later. Hospitality from the *gers* was always forthcoming, although some of the social rules of engagement often jarred with my Western way of doing things. It amazed me for example that complete strangers could freely walk in on a family home without even knocking, which we may consider a thoughtless act, and be treated with the utmost courtesy. Yet at the same time our hosts were cool and reserved compared to people in other parts of the world I have visited. Only at Batsagaan's *ger* below the blue lake was there any handshaking, and that only I suspect because I started it. Otherwise a host never made an effort to stand and welcome us as guests but remained squatting on one boot and motioned us to sit. The driver and the gentleman never removed their caps on entering a *ger* as they would have done in an English home, because if a guest takes his hat off it means he is intending to stay the night. The herdsmen shared freely their food and drink and always provided us with a small bundle of provisions wrapped in newspaper for our journey. There was never any thought of payment; every Mongolian knows that he will ask for hospitality many times during the year, so he is ready to offer what he can to other travellers. There is also an understanding throughout the countryside that should a traveller come upon an unoccupied *ger*, the door of which will never be locked, he can freely enter to brew some tea and eat a meal before continuing his journey.

Karakorum, site of the Mongolian Empire's first capital, had become a bit of a *cause célèbre* for me. During the frustrating weeks of my first visit, Bulcsu and I had tried in vain to get permission to make a trip there. Numerous excuses were provided as to why we should not. It was an area full of microbes which would be dangerous for us. There were no flights. There was not time to arrange it. But after our success in achieving a day trip to Terelj, we rejoined the fight with new vigour. We were finally told that it would be possible, but that the trip would have to be paid for in hard currency. The three-day excursion would cost five hundred dollars each. Neither of us had five hundred dollars so we never made it.

Genghis Khan had probably decided on a more or less permanent location for the capital of his Empire by 1219. It was on the site of a former Uighur settlement on the

River Orkhon, which, as today's official guidebook describes, was 'a very nice place which is possible to enlarge the city to be sunny all day'. The city itself was built after Genghis Khan's death by his favourite son, Ogodei, who was elected Great Khan of Mongolia in 1228. It was the first permanent settlement in the country, with food supplied from outlying fields, palaces, offices, and workshops making tools and weapons. Its temples catered to a range of religious tastes, including two mosques and a Christian church. The city was surrounded by a mud wall with four gates, each a trading point as William of Rubruk mentions: 'At the eastern gate are sold millet and other grain, at the western sheep and goats are sold, at the southern oxen and carts, at the northern horses.' At the centre of the city stood a magnificent fountain, designed by a Frenchman called Guillaume Bouchier, composed of an eternally green tree and a winged woman playing the flute. Beneath her was an assortment of dragons and lions, and from the dragons' mouths poured five kinds of delicious liquid: *airag*, milk, wine, alcohol and honey. But all in all it was not a very large settlement, William of Rubruck tells us. Not counting the Khan's palace it was smaller than his home village of St Denis.

Although Ogodei built his capital to run the Empire he remained true to his nomadic traditions and refused to settle there completely himself, preferring to wander around the area with the seasons. During the spring Ogodei lived in Karakorum until late April when he moved north to the lakes and marshes of the Orkhon River. In early June he returned to Karakorum, but it was not long before he went south-east into the mountains for the summer and then to the Ongiin River further south where he had his hunting grounds and a winter residence. In February he returned again to the capital.

Karakorum had just a brief history as the capital of the Mongolian Empire. In 1260 Khublai Khan established the great Yuan Empire and moved the capital to Khanbalic (modern Beijing) leaving Karakorum to fall rapidly into decay. Its ruins were plundered in 1586 to build a Buddhist monastery called Erden Dzuu ('One Hundred Treasures'), a colossal square complex with thick walls each 400 metres long. The only reminders of the original capital are a few relict monuments scattered around this monastery. Close to the wall is a granite turtle which used to stand in front of Ogodei's palace, one of four which protected the city from floods. A hundred yards from the turtle the modern Mongolian authorities have thoughtfully built an electricity relay station. Further from the compound, nestled at the foot of a small valley whose shape is reminiscent of a female vulva, is a stone erection that women used to sit by when they wanted to become pregnant.

Erden Dzuu is a key monastery in Mongolian Buddhism, since it was built to herald the revival of the religion in the country. It was also the largest, accommodating some 10,000 monks, and oldest monastery in Mongolia. It is, therefore, a tribute to its solid walls that any of it still stands today, since it was an obvious target for the Communists when they decided to destroy the church in the late 1930s.

Just how Erden Dzuu was 'closed' is not exactly clear, since there are no official records of the event. But an album of photographs kept in the lamasery shows the complex before and immediately after the closure in 1937. Stupas had been toppled, walls breached and temple buildings reduced to ruins, suggesting a military campaign with high explosives. It is surprising that the authorities did not raze the entire complex, like they did most of the other 700-odd monasteries in the country. Today it is a museum.

We approached Erden Dzuu through the modern town of Karakorum, a state farm of the Order of the Golden Star. It was a miserable place with wide gravel roads, faceless apartment blocks, a flour mill and power station that pumped thick black smoke from its tall chimney. As we walked into Erden Dzuu through the southern gate we were greeted by a haunting sound from another age. Tibetan horns were proclaiming the start of a service in one of the temples at the far end of the complex. With the new atmosphere of democracy, religious services had just started again for the first time in fifty-three years. Outside the temple, ordinary Mongolians in suits removed their hats to prostrate themselves on the concrete slabs in front of the temple. Monks in their red and saffron silk robes were slowly filing through the wooden doorway into the towering white building. Inside a small mêlée of Mongolians and a group of Russian tourists were slowly proceeding around the monks who settled themselves down and opened their books to chant. Small screws of newspaper containing incense were being handed to the visitors to offer to the golden statuettes and silk wall hangings of Buddha. Ironically, the newspaper was the Party organ, *Unen*.

All the monks were old, with wizened faces and stiff limbs. I suggested to Sainu that many of them must be monks who were thrown out of the monastery in the 1930s, the lucky ones who were not lined up against the wall as counter-revolutionaries and shot. Sainu agreed. He did not seem surprised. His attitude towards Buddhism had not been perverted by his teaching at school, where the guiding principle had been that religion was opium. Sainu's grandfather had been a monk, he told me, and he had taught him some prayers and doctrines in the privacy of his own home. This, apparently, had been fairly standard. Although Buddhism had been all but eliminated from public life in Mongolia, it seemed that it had lived on in private in many homes. Sainu's calm acceptance of its recent return to the public domain was reflected in the attitudes of many Mongolians with whom I had contact. It was as if Buddhism had been quietly sitting in the wings for half a century, waiting for the climate to change.

I spent most of the day wandering around the compound, alive with sparrows in the bright sunshine, and continually circled by an eagle hovering overhead. All the 108 wall stupas, built to honour religious events, have been re-erected. Among the buildings that survived the Communist onslaught are the tomb of Abdai Khan who built Erden Dzuu, and three temples to the Buddha as child, youth and grown-up. Not a single nail was used in the building of these temples, joints were either dovetailed or tied with ropes.

A very bored guide with a beehive hairdo and too much foundation on her face took us around the three temples. Each is adorned with larger-than-life golden statues, red wooden pillars entwined with dragons supporting ceilings intricately painted with scenes from the Buddha's life and times, and cylindrical silk hangings dangling like multi-coloured box kites frozen in mid-flight. The central altars are piled high with small statuettes, goat's fat offerings, bronze incense burners and silk-bound books. They are surrounded by cymbals, drums, horns and conch shells, peacock feather fans and fierce papier maché masks adorned with skulls. The walls are covered by heavy yellow silk drapes with Tibetan inscriptions.

I goaded the woman with the beehive on her head by asking how many other buildings there had been in the monastery compound.

'There were sixty temples of large and small sizes,' she told me.

'What happened to the others?' I asked.

'They were destroyed in civil wars.'

'When?'

'Long ago.'

'How long?' I pressed.

'Many years.'

I made the question more direct: 'Was it in the 1930s?'

Her eyebrows furrowed for a moment beneath the apiary coiffure; I could see the layers of powder on her forehead ready to peel off like flakes of paint from one of the murals behind us. Then she gave me a good answer with a very straight face.

'Restoration work was started in 1944 and is still continuing.'

I felt sorry for the woman; she probably had not been born when the People's Revolutionary Army was busy laying the charges and burning Buddhist paraphernalia. I wondered how long it would be before she was able to tell the truth about the desecration of Erden Dzuu.

My enjoyment of the monastic compound was cut short by the delayed effects of the previous day's *airag*-drinking. The Mongolian phrase for the call of nature is 'to go and see a horse'. When it is urgent you go horse-racing.

After Erden Dzuu we had one more location on our itinerary, a horseshoe waterfall a few hours drive to the south of Karakorum, but its beauty was rather lost on me because my exploits at the racetrack had left me completely zapped.

Our return to Tsetserleg was leisurely. We made several stops at small towns where the gentleman and the driver checked out the local stores. The driver's ability to find these shops baffled me. Occasionally the wooden buildings had horses tied up outside, but to the untrained eye they looked no different from any other wooden buildings in each town. Only when we stopped outside could the faint word *Delgur*, or shop, be seen in fading paint.

The stock in every shop was the same. There were basic household goods such as galvanised metal buckets, scythes and breadbins; a shoe section with a good range of styles, but usually just one pair of any particular type; a clothing section that made OXFAM look like *haute couture*; a counter with buttons, thread and badges of the national flag; the odd hat, and various pieces of *ger* equipment. The stores also had a food section selling large slabs of brick tea, millet, sugar, jam, biscuits, bread, aromatic balm from Vietnam, cigarettes and matches. They were Mongolian Wild West general stores.

We had lunch in one of the small towns, at its hotel. We stopped at several of these hotels during my trips to the countryside. Even the most inconspicuous place had one, and without exception we were the only guests. There are few tourists, and no travelling salesmen. When people go visiting relatives they stay with them. The only customers hotels have are visiting Party dignitaries, an occasional trade at best. We each enjoyed a plateful of *buudz*, a sort of Mongolian dumpling parcel containing small morsels of meat and a bit of chopped onion. There was also a jug of *airag*, but I declined to further my acquaintance with the stuff. On the floor lay a Kazakh carpet made from thick felt with fairly basic coloured strips of material for decoration. On the windowsill stood a cardboard vase of plastic flowers.

It was strange for me to see a herd of camels grazing in the green hills. They are animals I have always seen in the most bleak, arid landscapes and they looked out of place in the lush pastures of the Khangai. They took little notice of us as we ground to a halt, axle-deep in mud. Not so a squadron of huge horse-flies, who proceeded to torment us for the next two hours as we laboured in the mud, packing stones from the nearest stream into the tracks of the jeep.

My final day in Akhangai was spent at Tsetserleg airfield. The incoming flight from Ulan Bator arrived a little late at 11.30, but to everyone's surprise it was a cargo plane. Two dozen men set about the task of offloading some large crates, several bed frames and a piano. As the pieces of cargo were removed the gaps in the hold were quickly filled by waiting passengers who swarmed about the concrete landing square jostling for position. A rumour went round that another plane would be sent from Ulan Bator to pick up the spare passengers. We settled down in the dust to wait. My nose was peeling from the week's sun, and I occupied myself carefully stripping my beak. The driver watched with fascination. He pushed his corduroy beret on to the back of his head and gave his black hair a scratch, then crossed his eyes in an attempt to inspect his own proboscis. '*Hachinghung*,' he giggled, poking the gentleman in the ribs and pointing at my nose. 'He says you are strange man,' translated Sainu, '"*Hachinghung*" is strange man.' Soon several kids cottoned on to the strange exploits of the *hachinghung* and stood spellbound as I continued stripping my nose of its unwanted skin.

The Mongolians are very good at waiting. It is a traditional skill developed through the centuries while watching over herds and flocks. They were, therefore, ideally prepared for the socialist society that has been thrust upon them in which queuing and bureaucratic inefficiency are prominent features. Kids occupied themselves by throwing stones at each other.

The sky was clouding over and drizzle began to fall. Some of the passengers retired to the small waiting room with thick wooden floorboards and walls and a colossal stove that measured more than a metre across. It was midday and the gentleman disappeared into the adjoining room which was the pilots' mess and reappeared a little later to announce that Sainu and I could eat lunch there. Mongolian girls in white aprons and hats moved in and out of the kitchen bringing plates of rice, noodles and spicy meat with generous helpings of fat and a large metal kettle of Mongolian tea. The two pilots and several baggage handlers, who wore nothing to distinguish them from any other Mongolians, took little notice of us as we sat at their table. One pilot mentioned to Sainu that England had been playing well in the World Cup Finals in Italy, but the comment was not directed at me and otherwise our hosts were seemingly oblivious to my presence. Their attitude echoed that of all our numerous hosts in the countryside. I found it difficult to understand this apparent lack of curiosity.

It was a point I put to Sainu, who himself had not asked many questions about me or my country. Yes, the Mongolians were curious, he thought, but they were also completely nonplussed by me. I was the first Westerner they had met, and they were in shock and had no idea how to react. Their natural curiosity was also stunted by lack of familiarity with speaking through an interpreter. Mongolians are direct people, Sainu told me, and they like to ask direct questions. The result was lack of contact and the apparent lack of interest. This left the children to stand and stare, also in a state of shock, but without the reserve that comes with growing up.

When they had finished their lunch the two pilots left abruptly and hurried across the dusty courtyard to a couple of aircraft that had just been refuelled by a man with a lighted cigarette hanging out of his mouth. The planes were straight out of a First World War museum, biplanes with heavy noses and exhaust vents behind large wooden propellers. The drizzle had relented and the clouds were clearing. The biplanes taxied across the dust and took off.

We waited and the plane from Ulan Bator did not come. At about four o'clock the rain was cascading out of the sky and we retired into town to eat yet another meal.

If I had been locations manager for the film version of Orwell's classic *Nineteen Eighty-Four* I would have been delighted with the café-cum-restaurant we ducked into through the mud and puddles and pouring rain. It was decorated in that 1960s style of garishly coloured glass, false metal-patterned reliefs and chipped Formica walls that the Russians have perfected. In the centre the roof leaked a gentle stream of water on to a concrete square that in any normal country would have been a dancefloor but here was simply a concrete square beneath a roof that leaked. The atmosphere was thick with the smoke of cigarettes and the odour of damp bodies, and at the tables Mongolian Winston Smiths sat drab and miserable beneath the harsh glare from the uncovered lightbulbs.

While waiting for the food to arrive, I bought some cigarettes, a Russian brand called Kazbek, popular with Mongolians. They were the standard Soviet formula of a half-inch of thick black tobacco at the end of two inches of hollow cardboard tube. The tube part must be crumpled up into a tortuous maze to catch as much of the tar as possible before it reaches the mouth. The cognoscenti have a particular way of pinching the cardboard which the driver tried to instruct me in, but I failed miserably and produced my own brand of cardboard sculpture to smoke it through. These cigarettes go out after each puff. By the time you reach the end of a pack you are either dead or so bored you will never smoke again.

The food appeared on chipped plates and, as I started to shovel the gristle and rice down my neck, a half-smoked Kazbek crushed beneath my boot, I looked around this centre of architectural excellence. How could it possibly be, I wondered, that the Soviet Union, which was responsible for all this, had managed to send manned rockets into space?

The flight from Ulan Bator did not come.

We spent a few more hours at the airfield before giving up. We drove back into town past a factory with a slogan on its roof. It read *Quality is our Task*.

Sainu and I checked into the hotel in town and the driver and gentleman left us. It was Friday night in Tsetserleg. The only entertainment was a cinema so we bought tickets and trooped in just as the film was starting. It was Russian but thoroughly modern, about a Moscow schoolgirl who had fallen into bad company in the form of a crowd of heavy metal fans. The only elements that distinguished it from a thousand American films and TV series were the Russian cars; otherwise it had all the standard ingredients of the genre: drugs, rock concerts, a couple of grisly murders, car chases and gang fights. It was not even overtly moralistic. After decades of Soviet propaganda films, this was what the youth of Mongolia was now getting on the cinema screens. To my astonishment, the face staring out from a poster advertising next week's offering was that of Sylvester Stallone. *Rambo* was arriving in Outer Mongolia.

. 6 .

UP THE HOLY
MOUNTAIN

The next morning we were at the airfield bright and early to see whether Ulan Bator would be sending a plane to take us back to the capital. Yesterday's passengers had gathered for another day's waiting. Around lunchtime the aircraft appeared through the clouds.

The gentleman wore a suit and a pork pie hat and the driver had donned a fresh T-shirt to see us off. Sainu and I fought our way through the gaggle at the foot of the gangway and climbed aboard the Soviet-built An-24. It was more like boarding a bus than an aeroplane: all the thirty-eight seats were full and people were stuffing bags and boxes under seats and settling babies on their laps. A shabby hostess strolled up the aisle, not checking to see whether anyone had fastened their seat belts. The pilot arrived clutching his girlfriend whom he proceeded to wedge into the front row of seats, making the two men sitting there move up to let her squeeze in. Most of the lights in the ceiling were either on the blink or had given up altogether and all the air ventilation nozzles had been removed and sealed over with what looked like bicycle tyre repair patches. A pattern of scratched graffiti surrounded my porthole.

An hour later we touched down at Ulan Bator airport.

'You know the name of this airport?' Sainu asked, pointing to the sign above the terminal building.

'It means Good Deed Hill,' he said.

We collected our paltry luggage. It was strange how modern the airport looked. The same interior designer who had so splendidly fitted out the *Nineteen Eighty-Four* café in Tsetserleg had done a similar job on the décor in Good Deed Hill but on a grander scale. The walls were painted the deep red colour of velvet and they were covered in garish geometrical metal designs. Tserendeleg was at the barrier in the arrivals hall to meet us. He helped to carry our tent to the waiting car.

The Society had gone up in the world during our week away. The car that waited for us was an old black Mercedes with a different driver. The new man was dressed in slacks and an open-necked shirt, much more formal than the denim and baseball cap of the previous youth.

My status seemed to have been elevated too. I was taken, not to the rather rundown Hotel Bayangol, but to a very different place, some distance out of town.

We crossed a bridge and turned east to follow the river. After fifteen minutes we pulled up at a gate in a high fence that effectively cordoned off the end of a valley. The gate was guarded and the soldier scrutinised us before letting us through. He opened the heavy iron gate and saluted as we drove past him.

I asked Sainu what this place was, and he smiled.

'Only for very important people,' he replied.

It was Ulan Bator's number ten Downing Street or 'Downing Street number ten,' as Sainu preferred to call it: an entire valley guarded round the clock at the gate and along the hilltops. At the near end, screened by pine trees, there were two grand buildings in the neo-classical style that always makes me think of wedding cakes, where the Prime Minister had lived before democratisation. Opposite sat a modern low-rise block of apartments built for other high-ranking Party officials. At the far end of the valley there was another modern complex where the President himself had lived.

I was entering the secret territory of Batman's Batcave.

The Mercedes stopped at the apartment block and I was shown to my three-room suite. The living room had plush red carpets on the floor, a writing desk for important Party memos and velvet sofas that would have been ideal for the intimate chatter of a small cocktail party. The white-tiled bathroom was big enough for an ad hoc meeting of the entire Politburo, and the bedroom was large enough to swing a yak in. On the bedside table was a short wave radio, its dial marking the BBC and Voice of America as well as Radio Moscow and Eastern European stations. Silk curtains hung from the high windows and a fridge in the foyer was stuffed with drinks. How the upper echelons had lived.

The short wave radio was to be a very welcome change from the small plastic radios that were standard issue in every other Mongolian hotel room I had stayed in. These infernal machines were childishly simple, having just one knob, a volume control that ranged from very loud to not so loud but still loud enough to annoy you. They were usually set into the wall and impossible to turn off. They were permanently tuned to the State radio station which broadcast a staple diet of classical music and captivating news bulletins about the latest industrial output figures, outstanding productivity by comrade so-and-so of such-and-such a state farm, and enthralling details on Party resolutions concerning everything from the availability of soap to the poor knowledge of labour law at the Ulan Bator sewn goods factory.

Now the carpeted corridors and halls of the apartment building echoed with emptiness. Although I felt like a capitalist pea in a disused Communist pod, I was not completely alone. Dotted about the complex were an American couple, also guests of the Environmental Society, and two men from the British communications company Cable and Wireless, who were the advance party for an ambitious new satellite link that would eventually join Mongolia to the Western world. Occasionally during my stay the odd Eastern European appeared at dinner, but otherwise we were alone, the first Westerners to be allowed into the hallowed confines of the former Party hideaway.

The complex had an atmosphere very different from the hotels in town. It seemed to be just as overstaffed, but here they actually wanted to be attentive and helpful.

The waiters in the restaurant wore bow ties and white shirts and always provided five course meals of a splendour unknown in Mongolia. Each day the tables were draped with freshly pressed table-cloths, all the china bore the national symbol and the cutlery was embossed with two interlinked rings, the Mongolian symbol of family unity. Exotica such as honey, canned fruit, yoghurt and cake were regularly served up, the meat was usually of good quality and occasionally we were treated to some 'real' Mongolian dishes.

One of the phrases that had lodged in the waiters' vocabulary was: 'Water or juice?' Even though the 'juice' was usually fizzy lemonade, the courtesy was always there. There was even Western beer and Coca-Cola, although this had to be paid for separately in foreign currency.

I was also free to roam, although every movement was observed by the sentries on duty along the hilltops who reported to a central control with walkie-talkies. The valley was lush and green, a tranquil haven for wildlife. A herd of red deer roamed the pastures and marmots screamed at each other from their holes. Each morning I was woken by two cuckoos who maintained a cross-valley conference

all day long. Big black choughs with orange beaks flapped
in and out of the small grove of pines in front of the
Prime Minister's residence and magpies went about their
business along the small brook that ran from the valley
head. Butterflies fluttered across the lemon poppies and
bumblebees nudged their way through the forget-me-nots
and cornflowers. Wild rhubarb and lemon sage grew
everywhere on the slopes and eagles forever glided
overhead.

It transpired that the valley led up to none other than
the Bogdo Uul mountain, the former out-of-town retreat
of the Living Buddha of Urga. It was surely no mistake
that the Party had chosen this holy spot as their own
haven. The mountain was long revered as a most holy
place. One legend even tells that on the peak is the tomb
of Genghis Khan. It was not a location where ordinary
mortals should venture, being reserved for the Divinity to
walk and hunt in at leisure.

It was down this valley that the Bloody Baron and his
ragged mob had charged upon the unsuspecting Chinese
on that freezing February morning in 1921. The Chinese
had been holding the Boghd Khan a prisoner in his own
mountain refuge, safe, they thought, in the knowledge
that no god-fearing Buddhist would ever attempt to scale
the heights of this sacred place. But, true to form, the
Baron had gone straight for the jugular, knowing that if
he could rescue the religious figure this would put the
populace of the city on his side and make them rise up
against the startled Chinese occupiers. The thick woods
at the head of the valley must have given the Baron's men
perfect cover to creep up on the jailors.

During one of my walks in the valley I tried in vain to
locate the site of the former Boghd Khan's palace and the
oboo of the holy mountain. Mountains play an important
part in traditional Mongolian worship, rising as they do
from the otherwise endless plains. The peak of Bogdo
Uul, like many mountain tops, had once been a wealthy

individual, with its own personal herd and the rank of a noble, attracting a correspondingly large salary. During those days it was worshipped in a twice-yearly ceremony. One story of the Bogdo Uul tells how a rather corrupt lama of Urga went out to celebrate the spring worship of the mountain and was caught in a heavy snowstorm. He was furious and vehemently castigated the topography: 'I came here to worship you as a duty,' he cried, 'not because I wanted to. What do you think you are up to?' Then he condemned the mountain to a good flogging and ordered it to wear fetters which were fixed to its *oboo*. Later that year, still seething at the ungrateful mountain, the lama returned to levy a fine of all its horses, which he drove away, presumably to keep for himself.

Although it was a rare privilege to find myself encamped in this valley beneath such a powerful mountain which had managed to retain its importance through two such different regimes, the place was not without its frustrations. The apartment block had a strange feeling about it, of being in limbo, having shed its former role but not yet quite sure how the future would turn out. My Western companions and I felt somewhat cut off from the real world out there in the valley. We could come and go as we pleased, but we were always reliant upon our respective Mongolian hosts turning up in the Mercedes to ferry us about. It was about an hour's walk into town, but getting back past the guards at the gate was only possible in the chauffeur-driven limos.

The American field biologists, who had spent two months in the Gobi Desert studying bears, soon departed for Beijing, leaving me with the two British satellite men. They were an odd pair. Jim was a Scotsman, whose job it was to get the first satellite ground station installed. He was a sort of telecommunications troubleshooter, who sat at home in Milton Keynes waiting for the phone to ring and tell him where he was off to next. He thought Mongolia was about the weirdest place he had been in, and

Jim had been in a few weird places which he was apt to tell you about.

His partner, the sort of eager gangling character that Ronald Searle draws so well, was to be the ground station manager when Jim had finished installing the ground station for him to manage. He would be in Mongolia for at least a year and was approaching it with the enthusiasm usually found in a schoolboy looking for conkers. Jerry was terribly avuncular and rather absentminded in the way only the English can be.

'I saw a fox up the valley this morning, Tim,' he said over dinner. Jerry had brought his shorts and went for a walk every morning.

'Nick,' Jim corrected him.

'Sorry, Mick, yes of course. Big fellow, running into the trees. It's a shame that biologist didn't see him. Could have told me what type it was.'

Jim pushed his plate of half-eaten meat balls to one side.

'Don't like the meat balls, Jim? Mind if I finish them? Rather good, I thought. There's not much variety in Mongolian cuisine but it's good basic stuff. I couldn't find the deer at all this morning,' Jerry continued. 'I suppose they must have high-tailed it off over the hill into the next valley.'

There was an element of the *Boy's Own* adventure in Jerry. He had been a ground station manager in all manner of out-of-the-way places, from North Yemen to the South Pacific, and to every new location he must have brought the same schoolboy enthusiasm and his skill in Scottish country dancing. He had bought a Russian phrasebook from the airport bookstore in Hong Kong and insisted on learning the Russian word for everything he ate. Although there were no equivalent Mongolian phrasebooks to be had, he did not seem to realise that coming out with Russian words would not endear him to the Mongolians.

Jerry and Jim were waiting for their equipment to arrive by cargo plane from Hong Kong. In the meantime Jerry was entering negotiations for a permanent residence in Ulan Bator for the duration of his stay. This was proving difficult. In most postings, Cable and Wireless people are treated well by the company, Jim explained. They live a normal expatriate existence: nice clean house, maids, access to Western 'luxuries', membership of the expat club.

The trouble here was that hard currency did not buy a lot. No currency did. There simply was not much available in Mongolia.

No one lives in a house in Ulan Bator. There aren't any, other than the Prime Minister's pad across the valley, and although it was lying empty, it was not available for rent. But accommodation in Ulan Bator was a problem. There was a severe shortage of flats. The government was still intending to rehouse all the capital's population from their *gers*, so the waiting list for flats was about two hundred thousand people long.

But of course there were ways of jumping the queue. Jerry consulted the British Ambassador who put him in touch with the man who made the decisions, someone who was effectively the mayor of Ulan Bator. Yes, there was a place available in one of the Russian suburbs.

The evening after Jerry and Jim had been to inspect the flat they arrived at dinner with glum faces.

'You should have seen it, Nick,' Jim told me, 'it was a dump. Dirty, small, the windows wouldn't open. And outside there was a pile of garbage a week old. It was filthy.'

Jerry looked unsettled, but was trying to put a brave face on it.

'Yes, it certainly wasn't ideal,' he conceded.

'Oh come on, Jerry,' Jim insisted. 'Maureen won't stand for it.'

Jerry's wife, Maureen, was due to arrive soon, and the mention of his wife made Jerry laugh nervously.

There was a silence.

'We've got to bring them up to our standards, Jerry. There's no point in ducking it. They realise they've got a long way to go, and we've got to show them. You've got to insist they find you somewhere else.'

Jim did not mince his words, but he thought the Mongolians were a shrewd and likeable people.

'They're not stupid, Nick. There are one or two very bright people we've met. But they haven't got a clue about the outside world. They've got a few rude shocks coming.'

Poor Jerry was uncomfortable. He did not like asking for things.

Jim had told him to offer the mayor a few free phone calls once the satellite link was established, but Jerry was a stickler for the rules and did not like the idea. It could not be classed as bribery, Jim insisted, it was just something to help things along. But Jerry was still unhappy. I wondered how he had coped in the other postings. Mongolia was certainly going to test his schoolboy enthusiasm to the limit.

One afternoon I was driven into town to see the last remaining palace of the Boghd Khan or Living Buddha of Urga. The palace stands near the river in a wood compound and is preserved as a museum. Inside the compound are various temples and a residence which was built as a present by the Russians around the turn of the century.

This Boghd Khan, or His Holiness Boghd Jebtsun Damba Khutuktu, Khan of Outer Mongolia, to give him his full title, was the eighth and last reincarnation of the so-called 'Living Gods' of Urga. The first Jebtsun Damba Khutuktu was born in the seventeenth century, but had been furnished retrospectively with fifteen pre-existences, tracing him back to one of the companions of Buddha himself. He stood second only to the Dalai Lama in the hierarchy of the Tibetan Buddhist church. He was also descended from Genghis Khan, so that his potency as the leading figure in Mongolia was two-fold, rooted in both religious and nationalist feeling.

Mongolia's association with Buddhism goes back a long way. There is evidence of early Buddhist civilisations some two hundred years before the rise of Genghis Khan, but in the thirteenth century Mongolians started dabbling with the Tibetan brand when emissaries from the high plateau could be seen practising their art in the court of Khublai Khan. Mongolian nobles were attracted by some of the more wrathful Buddhist tantric deities who wore ornaments of human bone spattered with human blood and fat, and were often portrayed in sexual unison with female partners. These tantric practices were accepted without much comment by the practitioners of the dominant religion of the time, Shamanism. Shamans were a laidback pantheistic lot who simply interpreted these new Buddhist deities as special manifestations of Shamanic gods.

The net effects of the two approaches were very similar. Both aimed to put the practitioner in touch with the gods by inducing a state of trance. The Shamanic path to assimilation with a deity was usually to get high on hallucinogens whereas the Buddhist reached the same state through meditation and reciting holy texts. Hence tantric Buddhism was adopted in the noble courts of the Mongolian Khans, although it had little impact on the country outside the court, where Shamanism's worship of the natural world still held sway.

This state of affairs prevailed for a few hundred years until Altan Khan, a powerful prince who was descended from Genghis, was converted to Tibetan Buddhism by a lama captured after one of his campaigns. A great turning-point in the religious history of Mongolia came a few years later when Altan Khan invited a Tibetan lama to come and see him and bestowed upon this figure the rank of Dalai Lama. Hence it was a Mongolian prince who created this title for the highest officer in the Tibetan Buddhist church, and thereafter the links between Mongolia and the Yellow Faith grew from strength to strength. A few years after Altan's death his successor, Abdai, built the great temple at Erden Dzuu, ensuring the longevity of Buddhism in Mongolia for the next four hundred years.

In the mid-seventeenth century the religious and political links between Tibet and Mongolia were further strengthened. The then Dalai Lama awarded the title of Jebtsun Damba ('Worshipful Sacred') to one of his pupils, a young Mongolian. The boy was handed a yellow silk umbrella and told to return to his country and nurture the Buddhist faith there. When he arrived home his father managed to get him recognised as the supreme head of Buddhism in Outer Mongolia, and the position of Khutuktu or 'Living Buddha' was created for the boy. He and his successors were to play an all-important role in holding together the people of Outer Mongolia whose unity had disintegrated after the collapse of the empire, a unity that was to continue right up to the twentieth century when Communism took over.

It is easy to see why the first Jebtsun Damba Khutuktu became such a focus for Mongolian unity. Not only was he head of the Mongolian Buddhist church and a direct descendant of Genghis Khan, but he was also an intelligent, well-educated man with a particular talent for fine art. Many of his sculptures and paintings have been preserved for posterity in the museums of Ulan Bator. He has become an almost mythical figure, with stories of his magical and incredible feats having passed into popular legend. It is a measure of the awe and adoration that he was held in by his subjects that when he took a wife, against the Buddhist teachings of chastity, no one really took much notice. A legend tells how a group of nobles, who at first objected to this infringement of the rules, was silenced by the woman's evident miraculous properties.

One day while the Khutuktu was busy with a sculpture the nobles approached him to protest at him keeping a wife. The woman, who was known as the 'Girl Prince', emerged from their tent and the Khutuktu sent her back inside to fetch some bronze. She returned with a handful of molten metal, kneading it like a lump of dough, and proceeded to shape the bronze into a statue of the Buddha in front of the visitors' very eyes. Faced with such indisputable holiness the nobles left without another word. When the Girl Prince died, her body was cremated, but her right hand survived the flames and its ashes were mixed into the ink used for printing a religious text which was kept in one of the Khutuktu's monasteries.

The eighth and last Khutuktu also kept a wife, but in slightly different circumstances. The only stories relating to this woman's powers of enchantment tell of the special tent she kept for 'entertaining' various lamas, and the sordid affair she had with her hairdresser. The Khutuktu himself had wider-ranging sexual tastes. When he was not holding audiences in bed with his wife, sometimes apparently inviting guests to grope his consort beneath the bedclothes, he was busy getting drunk with various homosexual partners. One of his attendants, a man named Legtseg, enjoyed particular favour for some time, and they would swap clothes and reverse roles as part of their love-making activities. But the relationship came to a sorry end when Legtseg punched the Khutuktu in the face during a tiff, knocking out several of his teeth. The attendant was banished to a remote part of Mongolia, where he was buried in sand while the Khutuktu held an elaborate funeral service for him in Urga.

Even taking into account the fact that the history of the period has probably been rewritten several times by the Mongolian authorities, there is little doubt that the eighth Living Buddha was a promiscuous drunkard who was often completely blotto for up to a week at a time and only transacted state business in between extended bouts of sex and alcohol abuse. In his memoirs Dmitri Alioshin, a member of Ungern-Sternberg's gang, suggests that the Khutuktu also had a mean streak. As a child, Alioshin tells us, the Living Buddha once sprinkled kerosene on the head of one of his lama teachers and set light to it with a match. Apparently he also used to have fun with his subjects by setting bloodhounds on them or madly galloping on a horse into their midst.

But the private and public excesses did not affect his standing among his followers, who still gave him the respect due to a man in his position. The walls of the Russian-built residence were always surrounded by pilgrims who arrived from all over the country to pay homage. A holy rope made from camel's wool and horsehair hung over the wall, with one end in the hands of the Boghd Khan, who was sitting in his palace. Outside, the pilgrims knelt to touch the other end of the rope after handing a silk offering to a lama on duty. Pilgrims who had made this direct communication with the Living God wore a red band around their neck as a sign.

The Boghd Khan's poor behaviour and outrageous lifestyle was noted with disdain by many of the lamas of Urga however, but most of those who voiced their feeling publicly were swiftly dealt with, their deaths designed to serve as a warning to others.

It is unfair to paint the picture of the Boghd Khan as a complete degenerate. He had been quite a scholar in his time, having produced his own hand-printed Buddhist scripture which ran to no less than 108 volumes. He also had leisure interests. He was an avid collector. His palace museum is full of useful and useless articles. Several rooms are devoted to stuffed animals, for example, from all over the world. There are hippo and rhino heads, a polar bear and five penguins, a giraffe which has been sawn off at the neck and reconstructed inside the building, a tapir, puffer fish, toucans, alligators, several armadillos, two anacondas and four sloths. Many of these animals had formerly roamed the Boghd Khan's zoological gardens which he had set out not far from the palace. Other collections include gramophones, telephones, pianos, clocks, surgical instruments and various types of gun.

Many of the objects in the Boghd Khan's collections were gifts from foreign dignitaries. In one of his palaces the Living Buddha had built a garage which was crammed with motor vehicles of various descriptions. Few of them had ever been used. The first one was given to him by the Russian governor and, as soon as it arrived, the Boghd Khan sent two men to push it round the yard, in the hope that this would be enough effort to awaken the machine and allow it to continue its wanderings alone. But the car did not live up to his expectations. Next he decided to harness an ox to the recalcitrant motor vehicle and have it taken to his summer residence, where it sat until it rusted away. His other cars met with the same fate. Had any of the European powers thought of donating a chauffeur to the Living Buddha, he might have got some use out of his motor fleet.

The Boghd Khan was riddled with syphilis in his later years. The disease was endemic in Mongolia at the time and could only be avoided by complete continence, so there was not much chance of him contracting out. He had already lost his sight when Ferdinand Ossendowski, a Polish geologist, met him with Baron Ungern-Sternberg in 1921:

> He was a stout old man with a heavy shaven face resembling those of the cardinals of Rome. He was dressed in the yellow silken Mongolian coat with a black binding. The eyes of the blind man stood widely open. Fear and amazement were pictured on them.

The Bloody Baron enjoyed a good understanding with the Living Buddha, mainly because he had liberated Mongolia from the hated Chinese, making the country independent once more. When the Chinese imprisoned the Boghd Khan on Bogdo Uul mountain in 1920, he had ordered some of his lamas to effect his release in a special ceremony of exorcism by fire. Puppets were made of the Chinese commander and some of his soldiers, using real hair from the guards, attained at not inconsiderable risk, and then ritually burned in a pit. When the Baron's men appeared in the dead of night from behind the mountain to butcher the thousand Chinese guards they must have been seen as a divine response to the appeal for celestial help.

The Bloody Baron was also a White Russian, which was in his favour. He represented the least of the three foreign evils, the other two being the Bolsheviks and the Chinese. Although, later, when the Baron had displayed his true maniac colours, the Boghd Khan was to lend his credentials to Sukhe Bator and his gang in seeking support from the Reds, this support was exaggerated by the Mongolian Communists. The Living Buddha was not all that keen on Communism. When Sukhe Bator and the Red Army rode towards Urga to start their Revolution, the Boghd Khan pulled out all the political and magical stops to halt their progress. A decree was issued proclaiming that Ungern-Sternberg's White troops had returned to their own country and that the Mongolian government had re-established its authority so that it had no need of further outside 'help'.

The summons for the Reds to turn back was reinforced by magical ceremonies of exorcism performed near Urga to keep the People's Army from coming any nearer. A magical construction for repelling demons and evil influences was hastily put together and trundled northwards out of Urga with the Boghd Khan at its head. A band of Tibetans followed the procession, firing aimlessly with guns. But it was all to no avail. The Red troops easily routed the small force that Ungern-Sternberg had left in charge at Urga, and the rest, as they say, is history.

The Boghd Khan is still remembered with respect in Mongolia today. He was instrumental in gaining Mongolia's independence after 300 years of Chinese dominance in 1911, when he was proclaimed king. And he had tried in vain to stop the coming of the Reds in 1921. The fact that the new Communist government continued to allow him to be titular head of state for the remaining four years of his life has not been held against him. He did not really have any choice. The sex and alcohol must have been a form of light relief from the harsh reality of the fact that Mongolia was once more under foreign domination.

After the Boghd Khan's death in 1924 at the age of fifty-four, the authorities forbade the discovery of his next reincarnation. And so ended the line of Living Buddhas of Urga. When I asked Mongolians in 1990 whether they thought the search for the next one would be reinstated, they were understandably cagey. Rumours were starting to spread around Ulan Bator that a six-year-old boy had been identified in Akhangai *aimak*, but I found no one who could confirm the story. Perhaps in time another Living Buddha will be allowed to appear, or maybe such a figure has no place in a modern democratic Mongolia.

. 7 .

THE LAST DISCO

Anou threw her head back and laughed out loud when I mentioned Marxism-Leninism. I was quite taken aback.

'No one ever believed that rubbish,' she said.

Sainu had been threatening for a long time to introduce me to a female acquaintance of his who was apparently just dying to meet me. She was a friend from college days in Moscow, a well-connected young woman whose father had been in the Politburo but had resigned along with Batman and the others in March. He had been absorbed into the Party machinery and was now head of its publishing house.

His daughter was strikingly pretty. She had half-European features and bright black eyes which shone forth from an aura of sophistication and Chanel Number Five. She wore simple black court shoes and a black patterned dress that had not come from any clothes rail in a Mongolian *delgur*. The way she crossed her legs was provocative; they were wrapped around each other like two long pieces of snake and you could not tell where

119

one leg ended and the other began. If ever a fledgling Mongolian fashion industry mushrooms, this woman will be hot property. I had been trying to put her at her ease but had only succeeded in making myself hot under the collar.

I pressed the point about Marxism-Leninism since hers was the generation that had known nothing else. Surely they had been taught all about it in school and university, I asked. Of course they had, came the reply, but why talk about it? It was gone and nobody had swallowed it even when it was around.

'It is just Communist bullshit,' said Sainu, obviously pleased that he had remembered the phrase, 'and Communism is no longer functioning in Mongolia.'

I was somewhat nonplussed. I had brought up the subject rather tentatively considering that Anou's father had been until very recently one of the main guardians of the ideology in Mongolia. I had not wanted to upset her by referring to his downfall directly. Yet here was an opportunity not to be missed: an evening with the daughter of the former number two man below the President himself. Her father had been the Secretary to the Central Committee of the Communist Party. I was sitting with Robin's offspring. What had it been like being one of the Party élite? How did she feel now that it was all over?

Relieved, was the answer to the second question. Anou had not had many friends because of her privileged position. Now she was just a normal girl and no one could whisper behind her back. Her father had been found a job in the publishing house and was keeping a low profile. As far as she was concerned she was glad it was all over and the pressures of being such an auspicious daughter were gone.

We were sitting on the velvet sofas in my suite in the Boghd Khan valley. Sainu had persuaded me to buy a bottle of whisky from the dollar shop for the occasion and we sat sipping the White Horse from tooth mugs. I said that it felt peculiar for me to be staying in this place which just a few months before would have been unthinkable. Anou laughed. Yes, it would have been impossible before. This was a private place, only for very important Party people. She had been here before of course, numerous times, to be shown off at official events to visiting luminaries. But this was the first time since the changes. The reasons for her visits had disappeared.

It had been quite hard work getting her in. Sainu had wrestled with the problem for days.

'They will not allow it,' he said.

'Who won't?' I asked him.

'People will talk, it will be difficult.'

As it was, we had simply driven to her apartment and picked her up late one afternoon. Entering the gate of the valley had been no problem. The guard had given the usual bored and sloppy salute. At the entrance to my apartment block a few of the minions had given Anou the once-over, but no one had said anything. She had been a little tense at first, but now everything seemed to be relaxed. I just wished she would put those legs of hers away.

Sainu topped up our tooth mugs with White Horse, and I cut myself a slice of the Hungarian sausage that Anou had brought along with her. Did she not miss any of the privileges, I wondered.

'I have missed a holiday,' she said. 'I was going to Korea this summer with my father and mother.'

She meant North Korea, hardly the most exciting tourist destination from what I had heard about the place. Its Communist dictator, Kim Il Sung, has built up a personality cult for himself that makes the activities of characters like Chairman Mao and Fidel Castro look positively introverted by comparison.

'Is that all?' I asked.

'Well, we had to move out of the Party flat,' she added.

'They took all our furniture and carpets and we were left with very little.'

Sainu had told me about the flat. It had been a palace, he said. He had only been invited once, but it had obviously made quite an impression on him. Everything in it was plush, like the place I was in now. But when the Politburo had abdicated it all went. However, not all the clout of being a high-ranking Party member had disappeared in the turmoil. Anou now lived in her own apartment which her father had acquired for her. It is quite something in Ulan Bator, where accommodation is in such short supply and the family unit is still very important, for a single young person to be living alone. And her pad was just around the corner from Sukhe Bator Square, a prime location.

Not everything about being part of the élite had been a drag though. Anou had lived in London for nine months after finishing her degree in Moscow, an impossibility for any normal young Mongolian. She had been posted to the Mongolian Embassy in Kensington, considered by all to be the best possible overseas posting. But she had not actually seen much of London.

'The Ambassador would not let me go out alone,' she told me, 'and anyway everything was very expensive.'

Anou's job had been to look after the children of the regular Embassy staff and help out occasionally. But it had been a frustrating time, she said. The only opportunity to meet English people and improve her English that she had learnt in Moscow was answering the telephone, and on the rare occasion when she had to open the door to people coming to pick up visas. But she had enjoyed sitting in her room listening to Radio One, particularly the top forty chart programme on Sunday nights. Otherwise her contact with the country had been limited to a visit to the Natural History Museum and a day trip to Leeds University which has a Mongolian studies unit.

I was intrigued about the work that went on at the

Mongolian Embassy in London. What had they been doing? I told her that the British Embassy in Ulan Bator seemed to do very little as far as I could see. Four men and their wives to look after British interests in Mongolia? What British interests? She agreed, the staff in London had not done anything either. A few visas occasionally, some cocktail parties. That was about it.

In fact the British Embassy staff had been very kind and hospitable on my first visit. They regularly invited Bulcsu and me to dinner and social engagements such as their 'Thank God It's Friday' club at the end of the week, which involved drinking and throwing the odd dart in their bar underneath the Embassy building known affectionately as the *Steppe Inn*. But now that Mongolia was opening up and there were a few more Western faces around, the Embassy had become more businesslike. Jim had a less charitable way of putting it. He was a signed-up member of the 'What on earth are they doing here?' school of thought.

Out of the blue, Anou asked me whether I was married. Certainly not, I told her, but I had a girlfriend who was currently in Paris. Sainu smiled. He had been asking about Clare, and trying to make out why it was that I wanted to return home on the Trans-Siberian Express. The idea of travelling across two continents to be met on a platform in Paris was a romantic one, I told him, but Sainu simply could not understand why I would want to waste seven whole days on a boring train journey when I could fly to Paris and be with Clare in less than twenty-four hours. His logic was unanswerable.

Mongolians could never really grasp the fact that a thirty-year-old Englishman was not yet married and had not started a family. My answer that I had not yet met the right woman was usually greeted with an amused disbelief. The average age for marrying in Mongolia was slightly younger than that in Britain, early twenties for men and late teens for women. In the cities these ages were a little higher, but even so no one in Mongolia was fool enough to leave it beyond thirty.

I asked about sex before marriage. Yes, they agreed, it was not uncommon. Sainu told me that every boy knows about the methods for climbing into a locked *ger* at night to lie with the girl of the tent while her parents are asleep just a few feet away. But the Kazakhs in the west of Mongolia consider it very important that a bride should be virgin. It is traditional that the bride's parents fit out the bridal *ger* for a newly-wed couple, and they always take great care that the bed is covered in very white sheets. The morning after the wedding night these sheets are inspected, and woe betide any bride who has not made them bloody.

A Mongolian marriage partner was traditionally divined by the local Shaman or arranged by the parents. Both approaches have declined in modern times. Young people are now much more in control of their own affairs. But not entirely. Anou told me that she had been married when she was eighteen, to a man that her parents had chosen. She had never been terribly taken with the fellow, and she had got a divorce. It was not a popular decision. She was now twenty-four.

Divorce has become increasingly common in modern Mongolia, whilst it was hardly known in times gone by. Sainu was a traditionalist and did not think it was right. It is certainly still looked down upon, both because of the traditional attitude and because Mongolia's population is so small they need all the babies they can get. There are even government incentives for couples who produce a lot; a fertile mother is proclaimed a heroine of the State and given a medal.

I asked them about homosexuality, thinking about the antics that the Boghd Khan had allegedly got up to. Sainu and Anou looked at each other and thought. No, none of that in Mongolia, they told me.

Then Sainu thought a bit more, and said: 'Wait, yes,

there are thirty-three such people in our country, I have read.'

You cannot argue with a statistic like that.

What about bestiality, I wondered. Tales of Arab herdsmen and their sheep were by no means a total fabrication, and I was interested to learn whether the Mongolian herdsmen, alone on the steppe, were susceptible to the same lusts.

Apparently not. This one was totally new to them, and they were horrified.

The White Horse flowed and the Hungarian sausage was dwindling. Sainu was getting annoyed. He had told me I must buy at least three bottles of the hard stuff to make the evening worthwhile. I had refused. There was a half-full bottle of *arkhi* in the fridge, left over from an afternoon's toasting with Tserendeleg, but this was not enough. It was getting late, and there was the driver to think about. Anou invited us to continue the party at her flat. She phoned a friend of hers to join us, and we left. It was nearly midnight and the driver had been waiting all evening.

We sped through the night, the driver understandably a bit annoyed and eager to get to his bed. Anou's flat was in a block opposite the offices of Mongolian Airways which had a flickering neon sign on the roof showing an out-of-date plane taking off in what looked like a shower of sparks. The evening continued with more alcohol and some tapes of Radio One blaring from Anou's small cassette player. At three in the morning we went for a wander around Sukhe Bator Square and then crashed out, Sainu and I sharing the sofa beneath a yak skin.

• ● •

I was very glad to have had the opportunity of spending a relaxed evening with Mongolians. It had not happened before, due to the unnatural paranoia instilled in everyone by the Communist regime.

There had, however, been two occasions when I experienced some sort of social contact with Mongolians, not counting Bulcsu's evening with the mysterious writer Altangerel. Both were somewhat peculiar in their own ways.

By strolling the boulevards of Ulan Bator it is easy to see what the younger generation get up to of an evening. They hang around on street corners and patches of waste ground, throwing stones and breathing dust. Both are in plentiful supply. They are among the few basic commodities that Mongolians do not have to queue for (the others are sunshine and Russian advisers).

One evening during one of our wanderings Bulcsu and I found ourselves in what looked like a disused adventure playground down by the railway station. Metal dinosaurs ran down to a large empty lake in the centre of which sat a giant fish with its mouth wide open to form a 'tunnel of love'. A group of youths were enjoying this Mongolian Disneyland by throwing rocks at one of the fish's eyes. As we hove into view, the missiles started missing the target by quite a lot and landing in our general direction.

We waved and called 'hello' and a rock landed at my foot. Bulcsu had developed an instant formula for responding to this type of Mongolian welcome.

'*Be Anglihung,*' (I'm an Englishman) he shouted. 'Not *Oros,*' (Russian) and he spat on the ground.

This seemed to do the trick; the youths dropped their missiles and we walked over to them, and then followed the usual lack of communication thanks to the language barrier. We could only offer English, French, Spanish and Hungarian; they had Mongolian, Russian and German between them. Impasse.

'Japanese?' a guy with slicked-back hair and a leather

jacket asked. Bulcsu had studied Japanese as his first degree. A conversation ensued.

The Japanese speaker turned out to be the closest Mongolia could come to a wide-boy. He was well-connected in the Mongolian underworld, he told Bulcsu, and if we wanted anything normally 'unobtainable' he could probably come up with it. Religious icons, texts, silk wall hangings, you name it, this smoothie knew all the ox carts that such items might fall off the back of. But in return he was not interested in money. He wanted a good Japanese-English dictionary and any Beatles records we might be able to rustle up. He had taught himself Japanese and needed the dictionary both to improve that vocabulary and to polish up his English which was next on his list. His ultimate ambition was to get out of Mongolia and head for Hong Kong, where he dreamed of playing on the fruit machines and touring the whorehouses.

• ● •

Lamujab was in total contrast to this streetwise orientalist. She was a very sincere mouse of a girl whose face always wore the sort of extremely earnest expression that people have when they are winding themselves up for an important interview. Each time I saw her it seemed to be touch and go whether she was about to launch into a tirade against the inequalities of socialism or simply burst into tears.

She was another Mongolian waif who had been picked up by Bulcsu on one of his cruises round town. Lamujab was a sad and pathetic character. Her father had been a political prisoner during the regime before Batman's, and she did not like anything about Mongolia. She hated the weather, loathed Ulan Bator and felt horribly constrained by the system. She opened our eyes to the oppressive nature of living in the country under the Communists, which we had only joked about before.

Norbu had arranged a day trip for us one Sunday to a mountain on the outskirts of the city but still inside the militia check-point at the western end of the valley. Bulcsu persuaded Lamujab to come along with us. We met up with a friend of Norbu's from the Indian Embassy early in the morning. Lamujab was told of the meeting point near the State Library, but she said that she would not actually meet us, preferring to follow at a discreet distance. The poor girl was scared stiff of being seen with us Westerners.

It was a grim morning, cold and overcast. We walked briskly past Stalin who looked down on us with disdain from his plinth in front of the library. Lamujab was strolling in the same direction about a hundred yards behind. We stopped at the bus stop. Lamujab hung back, trying to look inconspicuous in front of a poster showing the Aeroflot flightpaths from Ulan Bator to Irkutsk, Novosibirsk and Moscow. When the bus arrived we boarded and Lamujab jumped on at the last minute, moving past us without any recognition and taking a seat at the back.

The bus wove its way through the industrial quarter of the city. We passed stylized graphic propaganda posters showing workers with broad smiles on their faces holding spanners aloft. The lines of chimneys were resting from their usual task of pumping black soot into the atmosphere. Along the streets crocodiles of workers were marching with digging implements over their shoulders, on their way to dig for Lenin.

It was not until we were some distance away from where the bus had stopped, and walking towards the mountain, that Lamujab caught us up. Suddenly she was overjoyed with the relief of being out of sight of prying eyes, and for the first time she almost smiled.

We walked across a pasture covered in yak's dung though there was not a yak in sight. The turds were strewn across the grass like brown polystyrene Frisbees on a shooting range. Inevitably someone picked one up and threw it and a fight developed.

'Who is married?' Lamujab shouted.

No one quite understood what she was getting at.

'It is traditional in our country to throw these at the end of a marriage,' she explained, 'after three days of merriment and much eating of meat the man ends the marriage festival. But no one will go so he must throw yak toilet to make them.'

After crossing the river, which involved much laborious dragging of willow trunks and careful positioning of rocks, we came to the foot of the mountain. Norbu informed us that if we wanted to pass water, now was the time to do it since the spirits of the mountain forbade urination on its slopes. So while Lamujab carried on, the rest of us all lined up across the railway track and ceremoniously pissed in the direction of the Soviet Union.

The mountain was steep, rugged and brown. Halfway up we came across the carcass of a cow which had probably got lost in a snowstorm the previous winter. We made regular stops to survey the scenery and catch our breath, but Lamujab was impatient and rushed on ahead scrambling over the rocky scree like a mountain goat. She reached the summit long before the rest of us and waved from the peak, urging us on.

At the top we stopped and drank Bulgarian apricot juice next to the mountain's *oboo*, to which we all added with stones and a few coins. From our vantage point the valley of the Tuul stretched in both directions as far as the eye could see. To the right sat Ulan Bator's power stations with small wisps of smoke escaping from their smoke stacks and blending in with the low-slung clouds which seemed to be sitting on the city. To the left the river wound its way tortuously across the valley floor and the railway track swept in graceful curves along the foot of the valley sides.

We clambered down the other side of the mountain and continued up a tributary of the Tuul to a derelict monastery. It was a sorry place, just four Chinese-style buildings left standing in a very parlous state. Beneath one of the roofs a slab of granite had some barely distinguishable old Mongolian writing on it. Norbu told us that the temple had been founded in 1736 and at its height had housed a thousand monks. It had been demolished in the 1930s after the lamas had all been shot or otherwise encouraged to give up their holy pursuits. Behind the four buildings stood a disused European-style building that had once been a sanitorium but now also stood empty.

We settled down on the grass in the old temple compound to eat lunch. Norbu had brought some jam sandwiches and a plastic bag full of spaghetti in tomato sauce which was gobbled hungrily off sheets of hard toilet paper. The sun was struggling to get a glimpse through the clouds and the wind was freshening. Outside the compound small dust devils twisted their way across the valley floor.

Lamujab was looking noticeably less perplexed and may even have been enjoying herself. She asked Bulcsu and me continual questions about life in the West. What sort of food we ate, how big our flats were, which type of books did we like reading, did we travel about in England, what did the countryside look like, and what about the shops. But each one of our answers seemed to drive another nail into the coffin of her life in Mongolia, although we were trying hard to give her as unglossy an account as possible. In a stupid moment of thoughtlessness, I suggested that she accompany us to the disco the following weekend and we could dance like they do in England. Lamujab almost smiled and said it would not be possible.

'But I have enjoyed myself today, thank you,' she said.

• ● •

Lamujab would not have been able to join us at the discotheque even if she had felt able. The militiamen on the door would not allow Mongolians to enter.

It also took some persuading to get Bulcsu to come with me the following Saturday night.

'I generally try to avoid crowds of people trying to enjoy themselves,' he said, 'I turned up at too many parties at university always thinking perhaps I might enjoy myself eventually. But of course I never did.'

I told him he was not going to this one to enjoy himself but just to say he had been. There was only one disco in Outer Mongolia, and he had to go. Bulcsu pondered the thought.

'I've never actually been to a *disco*,' he replied, 'and I'm not sure that I ever want to. All those sweaty bodies. And this one is bound to be full of Russkies. Very unpleasant.'

He was right. It was full of Russkies and it was rather unpleasant. But now I think he is pleased to be able to say that the only disco he has ever set foot in was in Outer Mongolia.

We had to push our way through a crowd of Mongolian spivs outside the door to the disco. Although they were not allowed in, they congregated outside like moths around the neon light of the bare hallway that led to the small bar which was Mongolia's one and only discotheque. Bulcsu and I talked loudly in English as we forced our way through, in an attempt to distinguish ourselves from the Russian and Eastern European clientele.

Inside the dimly-lit bar we were hit by a wall of humid sweat which throbbed to the sounds of Boney M. The nightclub was a small affair with a dance floor no larger than a bedsit surrounded by alcoves full of necking couples and a short bar at one end. The space was packed with about forty middle-aged Europeans at various stages of inebriation. Men with thickset faces and shaggy sideburns gyrated drunkenly into each other, with their saggy bellies slopping to a different rhythm. Many of the women, who had prepared for their evening out by slapping make-up on to their faces with a shovel and squeezing into dresses three sizes too small for them, were still learning how to dance on their high heels. One particularly bleary-eyed individual in an open-necked check shirt sat leering at a wobbly bottom that bobbed up and down in a brown corduroy miniskirt about four inches from his nose. The couple next to him were locked in a scientific experiment designed to discover the contents of each other's stomachs with their tongues. She was working on the premise that the way to a man's heart is through his stomach and he looked like a used-car dealer who was giving her spare tyre an internal inspection. Over in one of the alcoves a man with a face like a bowl of pickled cabbage was indicating to his date that neither his heart nor his stomach were worth bothering about. He was unfortunate enough to have developed a nervous disorder which involved scratching his crotch at regular intervals throughout his conversation.

Meanwhile at the bar a group of sponges were attempting to break the Russian national record for vodka consumption. These barflies all had faces like Victor Mature the morning after the night before, only they had not finished the night before yet. The Mongolian bartender looked baffled and bemused by it all, as if he had just walked into a Pasolini film version of Dante's *Inferno* in which all the demons were being played by Russian advisers and it just so happened that these were the people who were running his country.

From behind the line of barflies, Ahmed the Afghan waved at us and nearly fell off his stool in doing so. Bulcsu and I fought our way over to him. We bought drinks and wore out the conversation potential in about thirty seconds. We greeted each other, we were both OK and the music was loud. Ahmed was not having a very fruitful evening.

'Many mens, very little girls, not good.'

He swivelled round on his stool and just caught hold of the bar in time to stop himself crashing onto the floor.

'Meeting these mens?' he shouted, and gestured to two characters lurking half inside one of the alcoves behind him. To my surprise, two African faces smiled at me. I shook their hands and cupped my ear to hear their names, but they were lost in the noise of Pink Floyd singing *The Wall*.

I squeezed into the alcove and struck up a shouted conversation. They were two Ethiopian students from the hostel, the first Africans I had seen in Ulan Bator, and they thought the first African students ever. They were very polite and formal and looked rather bewildered by the alcoholic carnage going on in front of them. But what else was there to do in Ulan Bator, they asked.

Their story was bizarre, and a sad one. They had applied to do an overseas scholarship in East Germany with a view to a job in the Ethiopian diplomatic service. But a day before their flight was to leave, they were informed that the East German quota for Ethiopian students was full and that they would go instead to Mongolia to study. It was a fortnight before Christmas when they boarded an Aeroflot flight to Moscow where snow lay several feet thick on the ground.

'We had never seen snow before,' one of them told me. 'We wondered how human beings could live in such a climate.'

They had brought one pullover between them and no coats. When they arrived the next day in Ulan Bator the temperature was eighteen degrees below freezing.

They were taken to the hostel where all the accommodation is self-catering. Neither had ever cooked before in his life.

'In our culture it is always the women who cook.'

They had to learn pretty fast.

Neither of them spoke any Russian or Mongolian. Very few people spoke English, and needless to say there were

133

even fewer Amharic-speakers. Their nearest friendly Embassy was in Moscow, and no one from there had been to see them during the first six months of their stay. They would not have felt any more at sea if the Aeroflot plane had put them down on the planet Mars. To add to their induction nightmare, both had been in hospital with stomach problems three times since their arrival. But somehow they had retained their sense of humour. The end was in sight, they told me, they would only be in Mongolia for another five-and-a-half years.

When I tried to visit them during my second stay in Ulan Bator, the Ethiopians had gone home for a summer holiday. They only had three more years of study left.

But enough was enough. Bulcsu was getting anxious and wanted to leave. The Ethiopians said they would come with us since they did not feel safe on the streets at night. We downed our glasses of Cinzano and fought our way back past the staggering vanguards of Marxism-Leninism. The only positive thing that could be said about the smell of hard liquor and perspiring armpits which hung on the smoke-filled atmosphere was that it felt good when we had left it behind. We had seen the master race at leisure, and it had not been a pretty sight.

Three years later when I returned to Ulan Bator, the discotheque had been closed down and the party was over. In Moscow President Gorbachev was gallantly trying to dismantle the beast that had emerged from the ideological test-tube some seventy years before. In Ulan Bator the disco-dancing advisers were packing their bags and heading for home. For them it was truly the last disco in Outer Mongolia.

· 8 ·

LAND OF DUST AND GRAVEL

Time was marching on, and Sainu and I had our second reconnaissance trip to make. Tserendeleg had decided that having seen the Khangai mountains and surrounding steppe, I ought to take in the Gobi Desert. We would fly south to Dalanzadgad, a town of sixteen thousand inhabitants, capital of Mongolia's largest *aimak*: Omngobi.

The Gobi covers about half a million square miles of southern Mongolia. Contrary to the expectations of one of the world's great deserts, it is very largely a semi-arid zone covered almost entirely by grass. Admittedly the grass is very grey, dusty and tired-looking, but nevertheless grass it is. The amount of 'true' desert, of barren plains and drifting sand dunes, is small, only about three per cent of the total land area. But it is still harsh-looking terrain, and its position hundreds of miles from the nearest sea ensures that it is a place of continental extremes. In summer the temperature often reaches thirty or forty degrees Celsius and winter temperatures can plummet to minus forty.

The Mongolian Airlines flight to Dalanzadgad is the first of the morning to leave from Good Deed Hill airport. It is scheduled to take off at six twenty. While I threw on some clothes in my suite in the Bogdh Khan valley, I switched on the short wave radio in time to catch the five o'clock BBC World Service news. It was 9 p.m. GMT the previous day. Talk of a united Germany, Nelson Mandela in the USA and the worsening civil war in Liberia were the main news items from the other side of the world.

Dawn was breaking as I jumped into the black Mercedes. The cuckoos in the valley had already started their daily dialogue as we sped off towards the airport.

Needless to say, the flight was delayed. Sainu and I killed some time in the airport restaurant over a breakfast of mutton stew and bowls of hot tea.

Dalanzadgad lies about three hundred and fifty miles south-west of Ulan Bator, and the hour-and-a-half flight took us over a landscape that gradually faded from a rich green to the dusty grey of the Gobi Desert. Dalanzadgad airport was as Spartan as that at Tsetserleg, only dingier. All around, the earth lay flat and dun-coloured, baked concrete-hard by the relentless desert sun. To one side sat the town, to the other, far off in the distance, a range of mountains.

We were met by the Dalanzadgad representative of the Environmental Organisation, a short woman with an engaging smile whose name was Altangerel. It surprised me that this woman had the same name as the male author Bulcsu had met three years before, but Sainu explained that the name was used by both sexes. A man accompanied Altangerel, a middle-aged fellow who wore a red baseball cap with the words *Motherland Undor Wog* emblazoned above the peak. I never discovered what it meant. He was called Cerendorj and he was employed by the Hunting Organisation.

Dalanzadgad is made of gravel, wood and concrete, and

is shrouded in dust. It was a two-hundred-yard drive from
the airport to the centre of town along a concrete road
flanked by gravel. To one side of town stood the wooden
fences of the *ger* compounds, to the other the concrete
Party offices, a hotel and the town's central square.
Around this square stood a number of chunky concrete
noticeboards with glass insets covering displays of public
interest. In one there were league tables showing
Omngobi *aimak's* fourteen administrative sub-divisions
ranked according to last year's production output of meat,
animals and dairy products. Two other displays showed
long rows of black and white mugshots. One row was of
the *aimak's* best workers, while facing them across the
square, staring enviously at their prime position, were the
best young workers. With my rudimentary Mongolian I
was able to make out the best mechanic, the best boot-
maker and the best driver. From the youngsters' board
the faces of the best young cook, the best young canteen
girl, the best young welder and the best young militiaman
looked at me with a range of very serious expressions.

While Altangerel and Cerendorj went away to acquire
a jeep and provisions for our journey, I decided to get my
hair cut. The Dalanzadgad hairdressing salon consisted of
two small rooms, one where a woman did the necessary
with a pair of scissors and an anteroom where a previous
victim sat beneath an antiquated hairdrier reading a maga-
zine. Beside her was a very old bathtub full of scum. At
the entrance two kids were happily trying to shut each
other's heads in the door.

I waited for a little while, and my turn came. As I settled
myself in the chair the woman with the scissors looked at
me with a puzzled frown on her face.

In no time at all the tiny room was packed with Mongolian observers. News of an Englishman having his hair
cut travels fast in Dalanzadgad. Three small boys stood
transfixed beside the chair staring at the bizarre spectacle
and picking up handfuls of hair for inspection as it fell to

the floor. A couple of youths in military uniform with heads that must have been shaven only the previous day were positioned immediately behind me looking at my reflection in the mirror. Several women who may or may not have been waiting for attention to their hairdos jostled for position just inside the door. The kids had given up trying to measure their craniums in the portals and squatted beneath the sink to watch the show, taking their eyes off me only occasionally to pinch each other in the ribs.

I was a little worried that all this silent attention might put the barber off her work, but she proceeded to snip away. She had probably never seen so many potential customers in her salon all at one time. It could only be good for business.

The woman made a comment to Sainu who stood in the background, and when I asked for a translation there was increased puzzlement on the faces that were positioned all round me. My goodness, it speaks too, and in such a funny language. I was back in outer space mode.

'She says you have very strange hair,' Sainu told me.

I said, 'Is it difficult to cut?'

'No, just strange,' came the answer.

Fair enough, I thought.

It was a very reasonable haircut nevertheless.

Altangerel and Cerendorj had got things together, and at about 5 p.m. a jeep appeared outside the hotel. The driver was a slightly hunched string bean with long straggly hair that had not been combed for at least a month. He always had a rag in his hand and never wasted a moment that he could be using to clean his vehicle.

We got off to a bad start. The driver wanted to bring his wife along on the trip, but Sainu told him this would not be possible. Not enough space. This immediately put the string bean in a bad mood, and he took it out on us by driving at hair-raising speed through the narrow streets among the *ger* compounds and nearly crashing into a lumbering lorry full of bewildered Mongolians.

The jeep tore out from among the *gers* and streaked across the gravel plain at high speed. We drove in a straight line, with a string of telegraph poles on our right. Ruts and bumps did not register on the driver's brain. He just drove, gripping the wheel with white knuckles, foot down hard on the accelerator, staring ahead at the featureless desert.

After one of the most uncomfortable half-hours that I can remember, we pulled up very abruptly at a collection of smart-looking *gers* in the middle of nowhere. They were pitched around a central building with a very large water tank on the roof that looked like a Zeppelin ready for take-off. This was a tourist camp run by *Zhuulchin*, rather like the one at Terelj that Bulcsu and I had visited from Ulan Bator three years before.

We strolled over towards the Zeppelin building. As we entered, two drunken and sheepish-looking Mongolians staggered out, one of them clutching a bottle of White Horse whisky. Inside was a small restaurant with a bar at one end. The atmosphere was a bit tense. The waitresses looked at us with disdain.

At the tables sat groups of East European tourists, instantly recognisable as such by their styleless clothing and glum expressions. The food in front of them was similarly glum and styleless. At the bar another Mongolian was carefully counting out a wad of crumpled tugriks pulled from the depths of his *del* to pay for a bottle of *arkhi*. The bartender looked bored as he pushed the bottle of clear liquor across the counter.

The place had a peculiar feel about it, like a cross between the false jollity of a Butlin's holiday camp where all the inmates feel that they ought to be enjoying themselves but can see no reason why they should, and the simmering tension of a Wild West saloon where the

Indians have been let in to buy firewater and are feeling very self-conscious about it. If anyone had possessed a gun that afternoon the Zeppelin building would have become a bloodbath, and no doubt all its occupants would have felt much better for it, particularly the dead ones.

We found a table, and Cerendorj ordered beers. After ten minutes he had to go to the bar to get them for himself. He returned with three bottles of Radeberger Pilsner *Luxus Klasse*, all the way from East Germany.

We downed the alcohol and made our exit, leaving the crowd to stare into their plates of congealed chicken and rubberised rice. Back at the jeep the driver was furiously polishing the front fender with his piece of rag. He glared at us with thinly concealed loathing and opened the driver's door, tucked the rag in above the cracked sun visor and gunned the vehicle into action. Sainu said it was only another half-hour's drive to the place where we would be spending the night.

• ● •

We arrived at the entrance to Eagle Valley Reserve as the sun was setting. A couple of shabby *gers* stood to one side of the narrow opening in the hills. Two camels were gently tearing at the grass, and a dog snarled at us from its tether. A scrawny character wearing a frayed jacket and no teeth emerged from one of the tents to greet us. This was the warden of the reserve. He agreed to let us sleep in the reserve's cultural museum that was built in concrete in the shape of a giant *ger* not far from where he lived.

The next morning we were up with the sun. The Eagle Valley Reserve is one of the most frequently visited tourist sights in Mongolia, another place that Bulcsu and I had tried our damnedest to get to three years before. The tourists fly in from Ulan Bator, direct to the Butlin's Wild West camp we had passed through, spend a night or two there and are bussed up to the Eagle Valley to wander around and ogle the wildlife. But these trips have become such a regular feature that by the time the buses start rumbling into the valley, most of the animals have made themselves scarce. Hence Cerendorj decided we ought to venture out early before the tourist buses arrived.

The driver was already hard at his polishing as we marched up the valley in the chill of the early desert morning. He was too busy pampering his cherished machine to worry about wildlife. The camels looked up from their grazing as we passed, to stare with the sort of condescension that only a camel can muster. We climbed high up on one side of the hills and settled down among rocks blotched with bright yellow and orange lichens. Behind us the Gobi plains were laid out flat and dark like the ocean. We pulled out our binoculars and began to scan the hills for animals.

Cerendorj pointed to a distant hillside. Four argali sheep were wandering across the grass. Each had a magnificent pair of curled horns. The largest of the group must have stood four feet high with horns a good eighteen inches across. We followed them as they made their way across the slope and down into a side valley out of our view.

Cerendorj told us that he would sometimes spend a whole day tracking argali sheep with foreign hunters, waiting for an appropriate occasion to shoot. But they were relatively easy to track. Most difficult was a snow leopard, the pinnacle of achievement for a foreign hunter in Mongolia.

Snow leopards are internationally endangered as a species. No one really knows how many there are lurking in the mountains of the Gobi-Altai and Khangai ranges, but it is feared that their numbers are declining to the point of no return. They are magnificent creatures, with tails up to three feet long. Mongolia lost a good deal of sympathy in the international conservation world in the

mid-1980s when a BBC correspondent from Beijing inter-
viewed the then Environment Minister, who rather
proudly declared that anyone with a few thousand dollars
to spare could come to Mongolia and shoot a snow leopard. Cerendorj confirmed that some people still did come
to his *aimak* to hunt snow leopard; there were still plenty of
them, he said, although now a quota had been introduced
limiting the numbers allowed to be shot. Besides, he
added, their numbers needed to be controlled because
they were a menace to livestock. I agreed that this was a
problem that needed to be balanced, but would it not be
wise to be sure just how many there were first? It was a
project that the Environmental Organisation were propos-
ing to tackle, with help from the American field biologist
that I had encountered in the Boghd Khan valley
apartments.

Their task will not be an easy one. Tracking a snow
leopard can take many days. They are wily creatures, well
camouflaged and difficult to find in the craggy mountains
that they inhabit. During our time in the Gobi's mountains, the only signs of their presence were the occasional
carcasses of yak or sheep, unsuspecting victims of the
snow leopard's adroit and silent hunting skills. But experienced trackers like Cerendorj would be on hand to help
find them. He would be happy to apply his skills in this
way, he said. It was always a challenge to find these graceful animals.

When we returned to the concrete *ger*, the driver had
the bonnet up and was perched on one wing peering into
the engine. We broke out some provisions for breakfast
and tucked into a can of chicken in juice with pieces of
bread and some Baltika Marmalade, crystallised pieces of
marmalade-flavoured jelly in sugar. The first tourist bus
rumbled past us and drove on into the valley.

Later that day we ventured further into the Eagle Valley.
A mile or so into the mountains the valley narrowed to
become a pass just a few metres wide, flanked by sheer

metamorphic rock faces towering six hundred metres
upwards towards the clear blue skies. We followed the
small stream that flowed through the pass apparently all
of ten kilometres before emerging from the mountains on
to the gravel plains. The wind whistled through the crags
and eagles glided overhead. A little way down the pass it
became choked with thick wads of ice which never see the
light of day. The crunchy surface was dirty with rotted
rock debris. The trickling stream wound its way across the
surface of its petrified swollen cousin and disappeared
down a mini-crevasse into the pale blue depths.

The driver did not accompany us on our walk through
the pass. He was still being a misery and preferred to play
with his jeep. This time, when we returned, part of the
engine was in bits strewn across the grass. We obviously
took him by surprise, and he hurriedly reconstructed it.

We spent the evening at a Young Pioneers' Camp in the
mountains. We had seen the camp in the grey distance
from our vantage point that morning while spotting the
argali sheep; it was positioned on a gentle slope beneath
the rounded peaks. Its site was exposed and a howling
gale seemed to blow permanently. The sign over the
wooden entrance gate looked strangely familiar, and I
could not decide why until Sainu pointed out that the
name was Good Deed Camp.

Like other Young Pioneers' Camps, Good Deed Camp
takes children from the *aimak* for a week or two's holiday
each year. The kids pass their time playing sports and
being 'educated in cultural measures', as Sainu put it,
which happily turned out to be nothing more menacing
than competitions in singing, dancing and painting.

When we arrived, the children were gathered for an
evening roll call. There were two hundred and forty of
them lined up on the dusty parade ground, all wearing
white shirts with bright red scarves around their necks.
The wind was whipping down from the hills and across
the colourful assembly, tugging at the red flags that

several of the children held tightly in their little hands. A figure of authority was addressing them, reading out the rota for dinner that evening.

Sainu and I wandered around the camp compound. Beyond the parade ground there were loudspeakers atop each building and on tall poles. They broadcast the national radio station, the usual blend of classical music and news items. We stood by the fence, the wind buffeting our shirtsleeves, gazing out at the hard grey landscape. It looked pallid and ill. Even Sainu felt that this was a fairly inhospitable spot for a Young Pioneers' Camp. The one in his *aimak* in the Khangai mountains had been in a very beautiful setting, he told me, in a forest by a river. He had not been to the Gobi before, and obviously thought it was not a terribly inviting part of Mongolia.

The news came over the loudspeaker system. The main item was a real sign of the changed times.

'They say there is first conference for believers in God starting today in Ulan Bator. It started with some prayers,' Sainu related.

Cerendorj appeared with the Director of the camp, a handsome man in black felt hat and brown *del* with yellow sash. He explained that he would be happy for us to spend the night in the camp's guest *ger*. If we were ready to eat, dinner would be served in the canteen. We wandered down to the thickset building at the edge of the compound and trooped beneath a noble set of ibex horns over the doorway into the customary warm smell of meat fat. We sat at a table set for four, but the driver never joined us. A positively gargantuan Chinese sort of mock art deco chandelier hung above our heads. Thick wedges of bread and a plate of jam were set before us, and a giant battered metal kettle full of piping hot Mongolian tea was brought with bowls. A rich meat and potato soup appeared, followed by meat and mashed potato.

As we were wiping our plates with the bread, the first sitting of children crowded in. They were noisy and jostling to sit on the same tables with their friends. When they were settled and got stuck into the bread and jam, a relative hush came over the room. Curious glances were thrown in my direction.

• ● •

The driver had been tinkering with the jeep seemingly all night, and we had to wait for him to put his tools away before we could set off. The wind, which had been moaning throughout the night, was picking up again.

Today we were aiming for the wide plains to the south of the small range of mountains that held the Eagle Valley and Good Deed Camp. As we left the young pioneers, they were already getting down to the day's cultural measures.

We were in search of *hulan*, or wild ass, funny-looking snub-nosed creatures that run with a sort of short springy motion as if their legs are pogo sticks. Herds of *hulan* roam the Gobi plains, eating grass like a man eats meat. Hence herdsmen do not think much of them since they consume pasture very fast, in competition with domestic animals. Some are hunted by poachers who smuggle their meat, which tastes like horse, into neighbouring China. *Hulan* meat fetches high prices on the world market, apparently.

The landscape became gradually more lunar. The last blade of grass disappeared with the hills and we were left with gravel and dust and the occasional thorny bush clumped in a pile of wind-driven sand. The ground was made of iron, and there were few tracks. It was rough going. We had been driving for an hour or so with our eyes trained on the horizon when Cerendorj pointed from the front seat.

'*Hulan*.'

I strained my eyes in the direction, but could not see anything. The driver swung the wheel and drove towards the invisible creatures. Then far off in the distance I could just make out a group of half a dozen rather stunted horses. They were standing around doing nothing much at all. As we roared towards them, the driver swerving to avoid the odd bush in our path, the *hulan* looked in our direction and took off, pogoing away from us. We tried to make chase, but the animals were too fast. We could not keep up on the treacherous desert surface. We came to an abrupt halt at a dried riverbed, which had been invisible until we were on top of it and about to crash down the shallow bank.

We got out. Cerendorj suggested we might get a better view of the animals if the jeep drove in a wide circle and encouraged the *hulan* to move towards us hidden behind a thorn bush. Sainu and I made ready while the jeep drove off to encircle the six animals. The *hulan* were again standing like wooden models until the jeep approached from behind, and they started to bounce in our direction. But as they came within a few hundred yards they veered away again and took off at right angles. They were clearly not at all interested in meeting an Englishman.

We drove back northwards towards the mountainous shadows on the horizon and veering to the west. During five hours of driving, we passed one solitary *ger* with no signs of life save for a round concrete well with a wooden harness to which a camel is tied to raise the water. A little further on, a camel carcass lay like a half leather sack on the gravel. It had probably been killed by wolves. Its hide was still sticky, but the only eating left on the animal was for the maggots which covered its hindquarters.

To the right the grey mountains of the Gobi-Altai range stretched along beside us and to the left the gravel continued out of sight towards China. All across our view great dust devils rose up from nowhere and swirled their way in all directions to die out in an equally nowhere spot.

I'm not sure what I expected from Sainshand, a small town at the western end of Omngobi *aimak*, but it certainly did not look like anywhere I had seen before. The town was bathed in glossy battleship grey light when we hove into view, as the sun was getting low in the sky. There was not a blade of grass to be seen. Piles of shiny black coal littered the dusty streets and there was gravel everywhere. The resourceful hotel management had even put the stuff in the pillows.

A camel, pulling a cart, ambled by *en route* from nowhere to nowhere else as we entered the small hotel building. We were shown into two rooms joined by a central living area with the standard blue plastic radio attached to one wall, a table, some chairs and a very large television set. The woman in charge brought us a thermos flask of Mongolian tea, and asked what we would like to eat. There was a choice of boiled egg or roast egg. Intrigued as to what roast egg might consist of, I plumped for that, and got to work on the TV set to see what was on offer.

With some help from Cerendorj the television and its transformer were switched on, and we sat back to let the set warm up. The Russian commentary came first, and I turned the switch of the radio to as low a setting as it would go. Then in the top half of the picture we saw the feet of men playing football. I twiddled some of the knobs and the set went fuzzy. Then the heads of the footballers appeared in a narrow strip at the bottom of the screen. It was a World Cup match, all the way from Italy. For a brief moment we got the full view of Argentina playing against the Italian national side, and then the whole picture disappeared and we were left with the monotones of the Russian voice-over.

'Is football popular in Mongolia?' I asked anyone who might be listening.

'No.'

'Is there a Mongolian national team?'

'No.'

'Mongolia must be one of the only countries in the world without a national team.'

'It is not a popular sport in Mongolia.'

Just as we had exhausted that topic of conversation, the screen came to the rescue and restored normal pictorial coverage. It was just in time to see the referee blow the final whistle and the score, a 1–1 draw, come up. The game was obviously going to extra time, so I happily thought we might get a half-hour of reasonably exciting action.

Four-and-a-half thousand miles away, twenty-two professional footballers sat sweating on a football pitch in Italy. Coaches and managers buzzed around giving advice on tactics for the next session, and liquid was being poured from plastic bottles into open mouths and on to tousled hair. Some of the sportsmen had rolled down their socks and were rubbing their tired calfs. Meanwhile, in the gravel town of Sainshand in Outer Mongolia, the hotel manageress arrived with our plates of roast egg. It turned out to be an omelette topped with pieces of fried camel meat.

We sat shovelling the roast egg into our mouths as the footballers in Italy got to their feet and wandered back to take up position for the rest of their game. The referee signalled his readiness to his linesmen and blew his whistle for the first half of extra time to commence. The picture zoomed in on the ball on the centre spot and just as it was kicked there was a power cut. The black and white picture imploded into a tiny white dot in the centre of the screen and immediately vanished.

Sainu laughed.

We finished our dinner in the failing light of dusk. I was feeling rather grumpy, so I decided to venture into the town to have a look around. I thought it might be interesting to find out whether the gravel city actually had anything at all growing in it. So I pulled on my boots and went in search of a blade of grass.

The final shafts of sunlight were laid out at acute angles on the distant plasticine mountains. The sky was a very deep blue, and on it the moon was sitting like a projected slide of a white ball on a translucent blue silk screen. I walked up an incline to get a perspective on the place. A fat dust devil rose up next to a nearby *ger* and spun clouds of dust through one of the planks of sunlight. It bustled across the gravel towards a pile of coal and its shimmering veil turned black before crashing into the wall of the power plant and dying. The power plant looked as if it had not produced any power for about a hundred years.

Our hotel seemed to be on the main square of Sainshand. I only say that because it was more or less in the centre of town and formed one side of a square space with nothing in it but gravel. Across the other side of the square stood a line of notice boards with the familiar league tables of production I had seen in Dalanzadgad, although there were no mugshots of celebrated workers. I could not believe that anyone had ever celebrated anything in this godforsaken spot, except perhaps a chance to leave it.

And maybe that was what had happened. The town was strangely deserted. There were a fair number of *gers* dotted around, but not a soul in sight. I was still to come across any grass. Sainshand was like a deserted pioneer settlement found on the moon in a science fiction movie. It was as if the elements had taken over and begun the gradual task of reducing the evidence of human occupation back into the dust and gravel from which it had sprung.

Yet the evacuation must have been fairly recent. A woman was still cooking roast egg, although apart from us the hotel was also deserted, and the power plant had only just ground to a halt. Perhaps the lonely figure leading the camel cart when we first arrived had been the last evacuee, and the manageress would also vanish during the night. It was an unsettling town, and I was looking forward to leaving.

As I returned to the hotel, I caught sight of one of the final lengthy shadows moving. It was a head, but horribly elongated and covered in straggly hair two yards long. It had a nose that was as gnarled and bumpy as any on the most ghastly witch. I quickened my stride to reach the doorway, but the real head of the black shadow remained out of sight. I debated whether to return inside. Perhaps the football had been miraculously restored. But no, this was ridiculous. I had spent too long in the confines of the jeep, and my baked imagination was working overtime. I walked to the corner of the building to peer round, half-expecting to see a Shaman in full flight, come to exorcise the ghost town. Just as my head was moving to glance round the wooden edge of the hotel building, the sound of a heavy crash of wood against metal made my heart miss a beat. I looked round and came face to face with the driver. He looked up, just as startled as I was. He held a large gasket on the ground with one hand and a wooden club in the other. The jeep stood beside him with its bonnet open like a huge mouth.

'Sain Bainu,' I said, and he almost smiled.

●　●　●

I woke early the next morning and had to pull on a few clothes and my boots to make the short journey outside to the lavatories. They stood beneath a small knoll, a line of light blue sheds with holes in the floor boards above a deep pit in the earth just outside the hotel. As I emerged from the hotel, there was still no one in Sainshand. I rounded the corner, and there up on the knoll was the jeep. The driver was standing on the engine, looking down at me with the sun rising up behind his head. He looked ominous and menacing in the otherwise deserted town, and the picture reminded me of Clint Eastwood in the near final scene of *Dirty Harry*, in which he stands on a bridge ready to jump on to the roof of a busful of kids hijacked by a homicidal maniac. I waved at him and called hello. He held a large spanner aloft in response, immediately ceasing to be Dirty Harry and becoming a living version of the propaganda painting on the wall of an Ulan Bator factory. He must have been tinkering with his jeep all night again. Perhaps he was going for the honour of being best young driver-mechanic 1990. I made a mental note to give him my vote as I crouched down in the evil-smelling shed.

A couple of hours' driving took us well away from the ghostly gravel city of Sainshand. We passed through some hard grey hills from which we caught glimpses of a far-off magical mountain range made entirely of sand. The landscape was completely uninhabited, which was not surprising since it looked completely uninhabitable.

We came to the sand. It was golden and smooth in the morning light. We deflated the tyres slightly and skidded through a pass between the towering rounded peaks rising several hundred feet above us, to emerge on the other side to the same old barren grey nothingness.

Presently we came upon a *ger* and stopped. An extended family of about ten people crowded into the tent to watch us eat and drink, and it felt very good to see some fellow human beings again. As usual we, the guests, were directed to the back of the *ger*, the high status area, and to the left as we entered, traditionally the male half of the tent. The felt covering had been hitched up a few inches all around the base of the *ger* to allow air to circulate, revealing the wooden trellis which makes the *ger* wall. The by now customary array of bewildered children's faces stared at me from the opposite side. This family herded camels and goats, paying a part of their animals' produce to the State. Some *airag* was passed around, made from camel's milk, and I ventured to drink a bowlful, despite the horse-racing episode in Karakorum.

It did not taste very different from the mare's milk version.

We were not far from our destination, a broad green gash in the desert landscape where a spring gave rise to pasture grazed by camels, horses, sheep, goats and even a few cows. The strip of green grass was splashed with the brilliant purple colour of thousands of small irises. The elongated oasis nestled right up against the giant field of sand dunes.

The sky was frozen in glass all afternoon. Directly above as I lay on the grass, the blue eternal heaven was a rich cobalt colour. Just above the horizon on all sides the larger clouds had been made with an assortment of cauliflower heads and half-melted ice cream served with a scoop. Higher than these the cirrus had been spun from a type of fibreglass.

We put up our tents, and Sainu showed me the spring that fed this incongruous greenery. It was surrounded by a low metal fence to stop the animals trampling too close to the life-giving source. Perched along the top of the fence were numerous coins. The water tasted sweet and cold in the hot sun. It trickled its way along the green gash parallel to the sand dunes which stretched on for a hundred kilometres or more, Cerendorj informed us.

It was no surprise that the driver did not join us for a late snack lunch, but when I asked how he was, Sainu mumbled something with his mouth full of bread and sardines and pointed towards the dunes. Not far from where we sat in front of the tents the driver was crouched over the stream, apparently in deep concentration. I looked at Sainu with a questioning frown on my face, but as if in answer the driver suddenly plunged his hand into the water and scooped something up. He carefully took whatever he had caught with the thumb and forefinger of his other hand and popped it into his mouth. Fascinated, I walked over to where he sat hunched on the marshy ground. I peered into the shallow stream to see masses of small tadpoles wriggling their way through the water.

These were what the driver was catching for his lunch.

Sand dunes are amazing things. I never cease to marvel at their graceful curves and the multidirectional nature of the winds that form them. One minute the sand is hard and firm underfoot and just a superficial imprint of your boot is left on the surface; a little further on, with no warning whatsoever, your foot is swallowed up to your ankle and the walk becomes a wade. We trudged up the closest high peak and sat admiring the view.

Cerendorj had been guiding hunters for many years now after having been a Major in the Mongolian army for most of his life. He enjoyed his work, it meant he was often in the countryside. I asked him if he had worked for many foreign hunters.

'Yes, many leading figures from Eastern Europe have come to the Gobi.'

'Anyone I might have heard of?'

'Dubcek came once from Czechoslovakia.'

'Probably didn't stay long,' I said jokingly.

'President Tito enjoyed hunting, and Honecker from East Germany.'

'What did they shoot?'

'Argal and ibex principally. The Shah of Iran also enjoyed hunting in Mongolia formerly. His son who was in the army died here in a hunting accident. They made up another story to explain his death, but he fell from his horse and broke his head.'

'Do you hunt in the dunes?' I asked him.

'No, there are only foxes and beetles here,' he replied, pointing to a tiny beetle that was making its way industriously up the steep dune slip face in front of us. 'Do you enjoy shooting, Nick?'

I said I had never tried. I told him that there was a debate among conservationists about whether hunting was a good thing or not.

'Animals hunt each other, and we hunt the animals. Without animals there would be no food to eat.'

It was a simple logic and true enough. I remembered the traditional Mongolian feeling that real men do not eat vegetables.

'Where did you get your cap, Cerendorj?' I asked him.

'A friend brought it from Beijing.'

'What does *Motherland Undor Wog* mean?'

Cerendorj laughed and took the red baseball cap off his head to look at the writing.

'But this is in English,' he said.

I said that I did not know what it meant.

The sun was hot all afternoon, and Sainu said that now we had found this springy turf perhaps I would like to learn some Mongolian wrestling. We stripped off our shirts and set to. There did not seem to be any rules, or at least none that Sainu was going to tell me about. I had seen wrestling in Ulan Bator during the May Day festivities. The sole objective was to knock your opponent off his feet. It was one of the more tedious sports I have witnessed, involving lengthy periods when the two wrestlers seem to simply lean against each other, only occasionally punctuated by bursts of action.

The first time, we had scarcely locked arms before I was on my back.

'That's not fair, I wasn't ready.'

Sainu laughed. 'You are weak Englishman. I was wrestling champion of Bulgan *aimak* at my school.'

We set to again, and I stood my ground for a short while before again finding myself on my back. Cerendorj, who was watching the impromptu display, laughed loudly.

'He asks you have you never wrestled before?' Sainu translated.

I said, 'Not really,' and we started again. I tried to trip Sainu up, but this was an obvious tactic, he told me, as he made a lurch to try and grab my leg, which I repelled. Then he tried again and succeeded in kicking me in the balls. I folded up in acute pain. Sainu howled with laughter.

'Surely there's a rule against that?' I asked, doubled up in agony, but Sainu only laughed some more and told me what a weakling I was.

· 9 ·

BANG, BANG, YOU'RE DEAD

For supper Cerendorj made a large bowl of *bantan*, a heavy meat stew thickened with a bit of flour. He apologised that the meat was not fresh. It was in the form of long strips of dried beef, the standard fare of Mongolian desert nomads. Only beef and lamb are worth drying, he said; camel, goat and horse go off too quickly, but beef and lamb will last a year or more. It would certainly have taken at least that time to chew the meat properly before swallowing it, but I did not have twelve months to spare. Nevertheless, the stew tasted good and I congratulated Cerendorj on his culinary skills after I had managed to gulp down the last knot of leather meat. He seemed flattered, and immediately offered me more. We all took second helpings, and between us we finished off the bowl. Even the driver tucked in; he had joined us for the first time to eat, perhaps cured of his indignation and fortified by his tadpole lunch.

'We must put up your photograph in Dalanzadgad square,' I told him, 'best *bantan* maker in Omngobi *aimak*.'

Cerendorj howled with laughter.

'But we must be careful,' he said, '"*bantan*" also means "teller of lies".'

Everyone thought this was a huge joke, and even the driver smiled. Those tadpoles had obviously worked wonders.

Mongolian is a strange language, and there are many dangerous double meanings for the unwary to blunder into. One of the first words I learnt was the word for 'cold'. I soon had the phrase for 'I am rather cold' off pat, to offer to anyone I met after the initial delight usually shown on my rendering of the simple greeting '*Sain Bainu*', and in response to the usual 'How are you finding Mongolia?' that came next. Rather to my surprise and disappointment, the 'I am rather cold' phrase invariably put an immediate damper on an initially jovial meeting. It was always met with a strangely muted and surprised reaction. It was several weeks before someone, I think it was Norbu the Tibetan student, explained why. 'I am rather cold' in Mongolian is the same as the phrase 'I have got syphilis.'

That night the glass that had held the sky in position all day was broken, and the clouds rushed away as the wind got up to whistle through our tent. When we woke, the scene had been transformed by a cold, miserable driving rain. It was just my luck to come to the Gobi Desert on one of the ten days a year on average that it rains.

We all huddled into Cerendorj's tent for a cramped breakfast consisting of the usual cans of goulash and chicken in juice. The Baltika Marmalade was all gone. The driver was with us again, and this time he produced his own tin of liver pâté, like the driver in the Khangai mountains. It was obviously the standard fodder for Mongolian jeep drivers when tadpoles were not available.

We had a fairly boring damp drive that day, the only

highlights being when we came across a herd of gazelles who took our arrival on their territory as an invitation to a race. Unlike the *hulan*, the gazelle has a very graceful springy run. Fifty or more of the slim beasts sprang into action when our jeep sped across the plain towards them. They easily outran our vehicle, but for some this was not enough of a challenge so they made the contest more interesting by suddenly changing direction to career across in front of the jeep, often passing within a few yards of the bonnet.

There are two types of gazelle in Mongolia, the black-tailed and the white-tailed. Both have been declining in their numbers and in their range in recent times. Tserendeleg told me that there were millions of gazelles in Mongolia before the Second World War, but they were hunted in large numbers to provide meat for the Soviet army. They further suffered during a series of particularly bad winters. Today their biggest threat is the man with the gun. This is not so serious in Mongolia, but gazelles migrate across the wide plains from the steppes of the south and east across the national border into China, where they are hammered for their meat. In the eastern parts of the country, the annual thundering movement of hundreds of thousands of gazelles is said to be a spectacle to rival the wildlife migrations of East Africa.

During the next few days the weather continued cold and damp and we continued on our tour of Omngobi *aimak*. We were now north of the Gobi-Altai mountains and the landscape had become slightly greener and more hospitable. Small scattered herds of domestic animals again became a sporadic feature of the otherwise splendidly boring view. After stopping several times to talk and exchange snuff with nomads tending their camels and goats, Cerendorj found the place of coloured stones that he had been building us up to for the last few days. This would be an interesting spot to take my adventure tourists for sure, he said.

It was a source of continual amazement what an acute sense of direction the desert nomads had in a place which to me was so seemingly devoid of any landmarks. The men we stopped to speak to would crouch down to sit on one foot holding their horses' reins, and converse in hushed tones. They would scan the horizon with thoughtful eyes and say: 'Yes, I have heard of this place that you speak of.' Then they would point and we would be on our way. It was always a very matter-of-fact exchange of information. Not one of the cracked leather faces ever looked at me or Sainu, and the man would remount his horse and ride off as we returned to our jeep.

Our vehicle struggled up a dry riverbed and we stopped beneath a clay slope studded with brightly coloured stones shining with the drizzle that was still falling. Cerendorj jumped out and announced that this was the place. He scrambled up the slope and immediately started picking lumps of rock out of the clay and examining them. There were large gnarled lumps of what looked like agate, the stone from which Mongolian snuff bottles are traditionally made, and these were what Cerendorj was concentrating on. Among the lumps were many smaller rounded stones in orange, crystal white, red and green. We spent a couple of hours in the drizzle with our heads down looking at the stones, but I am ashamed to admit that my knowledge of precious stones is such that we could have been combing an undiscovered diamond field and I would not have known it. But they were pretty stones.

• ● •

The bad weather had passed, and the sun was scorching in a clear blue sky the day we looked at the dinosaur fields. Mongolia is a big noise in the dinosaur world. Back in the 1920s a young curator at the American Museum of Natural

History in New York led several very large scientific expeditions to the Mongolian Gobi Desert. His name was Roy Chapman Andrews. He was an explorer and a scientist, a man of bluff, bravado and drawn guns, the only approach possible in a land of nomads and brigands which had just come under Soviet control after a decade of uncertainty ruled by characters such as the Bloody Baron. A biography of Roy Chapman Andrews describes a photograph of him sitting pensively in the desert:

> He holds a 6.5mm Mannlicher rifle in his right hand and around his waist wears a loaded cartridge belt into which is tucked his other gun, a revolver. On his feet are dusty leather boots, and the sleeves of his rumpled shirt are casually rolled up. A worn hat, sporting a lone pheasant feather, is perched on his head, with just the right amount of tilt. The man is pictured in profile, his hard, clean jaw slightly elevated, his pale Anglo-Saxon eyes gazing off into the distance. Behind him rises a great eroded escarpment in the heart of the Gobi Desert.

There is a popular theory that Roy Chapman Andrews was the real-life model upon which the film character Indiana Jones is based. If you read his books, both scientific and popular accounts of eight years of exploration in the Gobi, it is easy to see how this rumour, true or not, has come about. His dinosaur-searching exploits are punctuated with tales of shoot-outs with brigands and face-offs with Mongolian and Chinese secret service personnel. The stories are tinged with a hint of humour from a man who was completely in his element exploring the wilds of Central Asia. On one occasion, while negotiating with the authorities in Urga for permission to continue his work in the desert, he was tailed by a security man. But the poor spy was completely exhausted by the end of the first day because on foot he could hardly keep up with Andrews' rapid sorties about town in his motorcar. Feeling sorry for the man, Andrews invited him to ride along with him in the car, which the secret agent gladly accepted to make his life easier.

Andrews always relished a good fight:

As long as bandits can rob defenceless caravans they maintain a bold front (he wrote), but they dislike exceedingly to be shot at themselves. Foreigners, as a rule, shoot much too well, and they do not follow the Chinese custom of running at the first sign of danger. Twenty Chinese soldiers, be they bandits or otherwise, to one foreigner, is about the proper ratio for anything like a good fight.

Andrews enjoyed being a cowboy in cowboy country. He was in Mongolia in unruly times, and ambush by bandits or soldiers was a constant threat. In fact, bandits and soldiers were virtually synonymous, he tells us, 'for a soldier usually becomes a brigand when a favourable opportunity offers, and vice versa'. But no matter who should attempt to hold up Andrews, his response was the same. One day while driving alone along a caravan trail he saw the sun-flash of a gun barrel on the summit of a hill three hundred yards away.

The head and shoulders of a single mounted horseman were just visible against the sky. Undoubtedly, the horseman on the hilltop was a sentinel to give warning to others in the valley below. I had no mind to have him in such a position, whoever he might be, and drawing my revolver, I fired twice. The bullets must have come too close for comfort, although I did not attempt to hit him, for he instantly disappeared. A moment later, as my car topped the rim of the valley, I saw three mounted brigands at the bottom of the slope. It would have been difficult to turn the car and run without exposing myself to close-range shots, and, knowing that a Mongol pony never would stand against the charge of a motorcar, I instantly decided to attack.

He drove headlong down the slope, foot hard on the accelerator, gun waving in the air. His charge had the desired effect. The horsemen's mounts reared in fright at the approaching onslaught. They had probably never seen a motorcar before.

In a second the situation had changed. The only thing the brigands wanted to do was to get away, and they fled in panic. When I last saw them they were breaking all speed records on the other side of the valley.

The scientific achievements of the Gobi Desert expeditions have a significant place in the history of palaeontology. When Andrews first left Beijing for Mongolia in March 1921, there was a belief that Central Asia would prove to be the originating point for mammalian life on the planet, including human beings. Mongolia, it was said, was the place where the Missing Link would be found. When in 1930 the expeditions ceased because Mongolia was becoming increasingly suspicious about ulterior political motives and China was deteriorating into a series of increasingly bloody civil wars, the original sensation over the search for the Missing Link had subsided. But Roy Chapman Andrews and his team of scientists had discovered numerous new species of dinosaur and very early mammals, whose remains had been lurking in the Gobi for seventy-five million years. Their finding of the first dinosaur eggs known to science sent the public at home in the United States wild with excitement. The actor John Barrymore, among others, successfully begged Andrews to give him just a few fragments of broken shell.

The week after we visited one of the sites of these momentous discoveries, I came across a modern pretender to the Chapman Andrews throne. He was a young man from the American Museum of Natural History in New York who, sixty years later, was about to capitalise on the new liberal regime in Mongolia and retrace some of Andrews' trails in search of new dinosaur discoveries. He wore his hair slightly too long and had a pair of small round academic glasses perched on his nose. He and one of his colleagues were drinking in the tiny bar of the Hotel Ulan Bator, which was really a dollar shop, but the counter could also serve as a bar. His colleague had drunk too much and was finding pleasure in abusing the Mongolian behind the counter in English, a language the Mongolian hardly knew. Perhaps it was just an unfortunate occasion, but the young men were not in the same mould as the intrepid Roy Chapman Andrews.

The last place we stopped before returning to Dalanzadgad was a town called Bulgan. It was bigger and looked more prosperous than Sainshand. There were several brick houses and even a few trees. More importantly, there were people wandering the streets. But the wonders of plumbing had not yet reached Bulgan. For toilets, the whole population used lines of blue wooden cubicles situated in strategic places around the town. In the hotel the usual contraption for washing was rigged up in the room. It consisted of a small metal container on the wall above a sink. Water is poured into the container and is allowed to flow by fiddling with a metal nozzle which has been cunningly designed to release either a dribble or a deluge. The sink drains into a metal bucket which requires regular emptying.

When we got to our room I hung my shorts, which were still damp from the days of drizzle, to dry on the window catch. A woman came in to make up our beds. Sainu suddenly looked very perturbed.

'You must take them down,' he said.

I was not sure what he was talking about.

'Take down your trousers.'

'I beg your pardon?'

I thought perhaps it was another of those misunderstandings like the 'I am rather cold' affair, but Sainu's English was infinitely better than my Mongolian, and he was looking terribly earnest. The woman was laying out the blanket on his bed. I motioned to remove the trousers that I was wearing with a puzzled expression on my face.

Sainu pointed to my shorts hanging on the window.

'Why?' I asked.

'Take them down or the woman is embarrassed.'

'But they're only shorts.'

I removed the offending article from the window catch just as the woman finished his bed and moved to mine.

When she had gone I asked him what the problem was. He told me that it was very rude to hang them there, but I could not for the life of me understand why, and Sainu could not explain. It was only much later, when back in England, that I learned that in Mongolia, anything worn or used on the lower part of the body is considered impure and thus should never be stored or hung above the height of the head.

The Bulgan hotel produced a pleasant new Mongolian dish called *baiser*. It was a simple plate of boiled rice and succulent raisins with a knob of butter. It is standard everyday food in the monastery of Gandan in Ulan Bator for monks who are not allowed to eat meat. When we returned finally to Dalanzadgad, where we had a day's wait for a plane back to Ulan Bator, I ordered it for both breakfast and lunch because it was so good to eat a meal without meat in it.

On the final day Cerendorj very proudly presented me with a hunting trophy, a magnificent pair of ibex horns. He had continually been on at me to bring my wife with me next time I came so that he could make her a fur hat, but meanwhile perhaps these horns would encourage her to make the trip. Despite my protestations that I was, as yet, unmarried, this was met with the usual amusement.

'You will marry Clare, and you must bring her with you next year.'

'Maybe,' I replied.

That evening, a dinner was arranged in my honour with the Deputy Executive Secretary of the *aimak*, the *aimak's* number two man who was also the head of the Environmental Organisation in Omngobi *aimak*. A waiter complete with white shirt and black bow tie spread a table-cloth over the table in the room that Sainu I were staying in at the hotel and brought supplies of soft drinks, water and the all-important *arkhi* for toasts. There then followed numerous plates of food.

At seven o'clock the Deputy Executive Secretary of Omngobi *aimak* arrived. I had been expecting a po-faced Party man in a stiff Crimplene suit covered in small enamel badges of Lenin, but he was nothing of the sort. He had a friendly face with a pale complexion and a slightly nervous smile. He wore slacks and open sandals and a T-shirt buttoned up to the neck, with not an enamel badge in sight.

We waded through a large meal of cucumbers and tomatoes, cold lamb, and an interesting pancake affair stuffed with meat in a sweet sauce, followed by more meat but this time with rice and pickled slices of carrot. The conversation was amazingly frank and open. The Deputy Executive Secretary told me that he welcomed the political changes that had happened in Mongolia. I thought to myself: 'Well you have to, don't you?' Then he said that we would not have been able to sit and have this conversation a few years ago, and I agreed. Since he had raised the subject, I added that it had to be a good thing that people were now able to say what they thought. As a visitor I was finding Mongolia today a much more pleasant and relaxed country than three years before. For a moment, it seemed that I had overdone things. Both Sainu and the Deputy Executive Secretary were looking uncomfortable.

Then the Party man smiled very gently and genuinely, and said: 'The system was wrong and the changes were needed. I have been Deputy Executive Secretary of this *aimak* for fifteen years, I am a classic example of the bureaucratic system.'

I nearly fell off my chair.

'Will you remain Deputy Executive Secretary of this *aimak*?' I asked him.

He told me that he was standing for parliament in the forthcoming elections, for one of the seats in the Little Hural.

'I have never been nominated before,' he said. 'It is there that I can do the best work for Omngobi *aimak*.'

I thought to myself that this man must have upset someone somewhere in the Party hierarchy, since he could not have been much over forty and had obviously been a bit of a whizzkid to make Deputy Executive Secretary in his mid-twenties. Perhaps the changes would enable him to progress further.

'And if you are not elected?' I asked. 'What then? Is there a phrase in Mongolia like the one they have in China? Someone with a government or Party job is said to have an 'iron rice bowl', a job guaranteed for life.'

'We do not have a saying like this one, but certainly I will always have a job, the Party will look after me.'

The Deputy Executive Secretary smiled and put his hand on Cerendorj's shoulder.

'And this man, too, must keep his job. When you are bringing visitors from England we need good guides like Cerendorj. He needs to be out in the open. He has been sitting at the table of bureaucracy for too long.'

The conversation took a serious turn. The Deputy Executive Secretary told me that he hoped his people would not expect too much too soon. He welcomed democracy, but he was afraid of anarchy as the changes were put into action.

'Whatever the Party policy would be, I want to push the market economy forward here in Omngobi *aimak*. Tomorrow I am welcoming a group of Chinese and Mongolians from Inner Mongolia who will come to talk about trade relations.'

But he was worried about certain things, he confessed. Unemployment was a problem in England, he thought. How does this happen and what was done about it? It was a problem the Mongolians did not know about.

I told him that if someone did not do his job properly then his employer could sack him. The Deputy Executive Secretary looked horrified.

'But how can he live? What about his family?'

'There is a social security system.'

'But you cannot do this to a person!' he exclaimed.

'But in the market economy, where businesses make profits, if employees do no work this is bad for the business. They are being paid a wage, but they do no work. They should be sacked. They can look for another job.'

This was met by a stunned silence.

I added: 'Many of the waitresses in the restaurants I have been in here in Mongolia would be sacked in England. They don't do anything.'

Sainu jumped to the waitresses' rescue.

'This is because they are paid too little,' he said.

'Yes, and if they were working in a market economy they would receive tips, so that if they did a good job their guests would pay them more. Therefore they would have an incentive to work well.'

The point took a little time to sink in as it was translated. The Mongolians nodded their heads.

'It will take time for our people to get accustomed to this new way of doing things,' Sainu said.

When the Deputy Executive Secretary of Omngobi *aimak* took his leave, he thanked me.

'I have always liked international relations and co-operation,' he said, 'it is just that before I was not able to express this opinion.'

I wished him well. He and his people had a difficult time ahead.

● ● ●

From the window of the plane that took Sainu and me back to Ulan Bator the gravel plains of the Gobi took on the colour and consistency of a rice pudding that had been almost burnt. The occasional hills were like air bubbles in the surface, although their tops shone in the early morning sun like the elbows of a well-worn leather coat.

My mind wandered back to another trip I had made to the Gobi three years before. While Bulcsu and I were trying in vain to be allowed out of the capital through the usual dead-end channels of *Zhuulchin*, I was miraculously taken on a whirlwind thirty-six hour visit to a town north of Dalanzadgad, a place called Mandalgobi, capital of the *aimak* known as Dundgobi. Needless to say, Bulcsu was disgusted with my luck.

Just how it was organised I shall never know, suffice to say that the man named Dembereldorj at the Institute of Hydrometeorology had some magical influence over the powers that were. Although he had suggested a trip himself, I was never really expecting it to materialise. Then one morning, as I was getting ready to walk to the Institute, the phone rang. It was Dembereldorj.

'Your trip to the Gobi will happen today,' he said. 'I cannot come, so you will go with Tsetseg. I hope you have a good time. A car will pick you up from the hotel in fifteen minutes.' And then he hung up.

I had just enough time to throw a few things into a bag and grab my sheepskin coat. I did not have a clue where

I was going or how long I would be away. I left a hurriedly scribbled note for Bulcsu at the reception desk, apologising for getting out of Ulan Bator without him, and jumped into the black Volga that was already waiting in the street outside. The tyres screeched as we took off for the airport.

My standing during this magical mystery tour to the Gobi Desert reflected a strange mixture of the red carpet treatment due to a VIP and the close security needed for a dangerous prisoner in transit. Tsetseg had gained a certain rather grudging respect for me since someone above her in the hierarchy clearly thought I was important enough to warrant this unscheduled and what seemed to her rather rash and unnecessary trip. At Ulan Bator airport we were allowed to wait for our flight in a private departure room usually reserved for Party people, and the crowd of other passengers on our flight was made to hang around the gangway on the tarmac to let me board the aircraft first. The stewardess handed me a picture book called *Socialist Mongolia* to read during the forty-minute flight.

But when we had driven the short distance from Mandalgobi airstrip to the town's guest house, past a dilapidated hoarding depicting a nuclear mushroom cloud with the words *Nuclear Power No Thanks* scrawled across it, my status changed from VIP to dangerous prisoner. Tsetseg showed me to my room and told me not to leave it on any account. Someone will bring you breakfast, she said.

'Is there no restaurant?' I asked.

'Yes, but you must eat in your room,' she ordered. She shut the door and disappeared.

Outside my window the wind funnelled clouds of dust along the street. Beyond a row of *gers* a hundred yards away, the Gobi plain stretched into the endless distance, grey, dull and featureless. I wondered what difference a nuclear explosion would make to this sort of landscape. A man rode by on a Bactrian camel, his *del* buttoned up tight against the elements. It was mid-May and five below zero.

The room was quite comfortable, with plastic mock-wooden plank walls. It contained a large table and chair, a TV set that looked somewhat out of place, and a smaller table with telephone and a red directory of numbers that measured two inches by four inches. I flicked through the ninety-odd pages. There were an average of four numbers per page. Attached to this room were a toilet and shower and a small bedroom.

As I stood surveying the scene and pinching myself to remind me that this was not a dream but real life in Mandalgobi, Outer Mongolia, the door opened behind me.

A Mongolian walked straight into my room and started to speak to me in Russian. I told him that I was English.

'Do you speak Russian?' he asked in perfect English.

'No,' I replied.

He brushed past me and sat down next to the small table on which the telephone sat. He picked up the receiver and dialled three numbers.

Two clicks were audible. He replaced the receiver. The man said something in Mongolian, and I repeated that I was English and could not speak Mongolian. He smiled and raised his hands as if he was holding a rifle, squinting his eye to aim at my throat.

'Bang. Bang,' he said in English, and burst out laughing.

The clouds of dust outside were still billowing past the window. The man picked up the receiver again and dialled the three numbers.

Click, click, click. He left without another word.

The telephone rang six times during the course of the morning. Each time I answered, the line went dead.

A couple of minutes after the man with the rifle had left, a young woman brought my breakfast, a plate of beef and rice, some bread, a bowl of mutton soup and a thermos flask of hot water with tea. The woman did not look at me and did not respond to my rendering of the Mongolian for 'hello' and 'thank you' – a Mongolian automaid.

During the course of the meal my door was opened on four occasions. There was no lock. Each time a different face looked at me from the doorway, a penetrating stare from deep brown eyes, and then disappeared. I felt like the proverbial condemned man eating a hearty breakfast.

My mind started wandering wildly. Here I was on the edge of the Gobi Desert in Outer Mongolia; no one knew exactly where I was or how long I was supposed to be there. In fact neither did I. All I had written to Bulcsu was: 'Gone to the Gobi, don't know how long for. Sorry. See you soon.' I did not even know what I was supposed to be doing here in Mandalgobi. What was there to do in Mandalgobi? Nothing that I could see. I felt like panicking. If the Mongolian authorities had decided to make me disappear, they had done a very professional job: the last-minute phone call, not telling me where I was going, giving me the red carpet treatment *en route*. And I had made their life easy by going along with it every step of the way. And now the nightmare was beginning. You do read every now and again of academics being held in some awful jail in a far-off place for no reason.

Just at that moment there was a knock at the door and it was opened again. Tsetseg walked in.

'May I enter?' she enquired, but she was already inside the room.

'Tsetseg, what are we doing here?'

'We are going to inspect a meteorological station,' she replied. 'Are you ready? Did you have good breakfast?'

We drove in a jeep the seventy kilometres to a place called Gurvansayhan. It was a landscape of wide-open nothingness covered in inedible-looking grass. I was disappointed by the grass and said so.

'This isn't real desert,' I complained.

Tsetseg looked very puzzled.

She said, 'This is Gobi.'

Gurvansayhan was, of course, even more remote than Mandalgobi. It was a collection of about fifty *gers*, a couple of brick buildings and a blindfolded camel endlessly circling a well to raise water. The scene was surrounded by dirt and nothingness.

The meteorological station was in one of the brick buildings, and four women in silk *dels* and a man in a western suit showed me their Stevenson screen and other equipment. Readings are taken every three hours, they explained, and telephoned to Mandalgobi.

Outside their office stood a large propeller three or four metres above the ground, a wind machine to generate electricity. It was a gift from their friends in the Soviet Union, the man in the suit explained, but it had broken down and they could not get any spare parts.

Tsetseg giggled nervously at my account of the morning's incidents in my room as we bounced our way back on the two-hour drive to Mandalgobi.

'Country people are curious,' was all she could come up with, and she quickly turned the conversation towards the condition of the British proletariat.

'How may we observe the conditions of peasants in England?'

I explained that there were no peasants in England.

'For example,' she continued unimpressed, 'I have read in newspaper that in your country people must pay much money for schooling. How poor people, peasant, go to school?'

I began to explain, but she took no notice, butting in to give me some other facts about bloody peasants in England. Her information was from *Unen*, the Party newspaper, so there was not any question about its accuracy. I was getting cross. I counted to three and began again; she listened, but I do not think she believed me. It was impossible to get through to her. I could imagine her

172

sitting in a schoolroom somewhere in Moscow being trained to deal with lying Western capitalists like me.

• ● •

And what a good job all that is over, I thought to myself as the Mongolian Airlines flight touched down at Good Deed Hill airport and Sainu and I were whisked away into the capital, this time in a brand new Mercedes-Benz. The Environmental Organisation seemed to have really got the hang of this market economy business.

· 10 ·

EVENTS AND
NON-EVENTS

Back in Ulan Bator, things were gearing up for the forth-coming elections. People on the streets could be seen reading the opposition parties' news-sheets and carefully studying their leaflets, many of which depicted candidates praying in front of Buddhist monks. The readiness of religion to resurface in the changed political climate was clearly an important consideration, and all the opposition party rallies started with a few prayers. Not all the lobby-ing and campaigning was of this orthodox kind, though: one enterprising party had hired a rock band to tour the *ger* compounds on the back of a truck and sing songs with political and social overtones.

The fact that opposition parties were being allowed to print and circulate their own news-sheets was a major step forward in itself. When I asked, on my first visit, to photocopy an academic paper, I had been met with blank and embarrassed looks. It was not that photocopiers had not reached the Mongolian People's Republic. They were there all right, but these machines were potentially very dangerous weapons if used by the wrong people. Hence they were carefully guarded, and all requests for their use were very painstakingly scrutinised. Needless to say, the request had to be made by means of innumerable forms, and the article to be copied submitted for inspection. The ridiculous process kept an entire special division of the Interior Ministry happily occupied in their bureaucratic work. And of course this special division delighted in their task, keeping the offending pieces of paper for as long as possible before issuing a rejection. When I had asked how long it might take to get permission to copy a seemingly innocuous article entitled *The Soil Geographic Zoning of Mongolia*, I had been told one year.

'One year!'

'Yes.'

'Twelve months?'

'At least.'

I paused to let this piece of information sink in.

'So if I was to fill in these forms now, I would not get an answer until this time next year at the earliest?'

'That's right.'

'And even then the answer might be "No"?'

'Correct.'

The loosening-up of Mongolian society had been a rapid process. While the political ferment was quickly brewing in countries such as Hungary, East Germany and Czechoslovakia during the summer of 1989, the Communist government in Ulan Bator was also considering experimentation with a multi-party system, semi-private farming and a freer press in the new atmosphere of glasnost, or *il tod* as the Mongolians know it.

Mongolians were also beginning to examine publicly some of the seamier sides of their country's past, such as the widespread disappearances of various people during the Stalinist purges of the 1930s, events that everyone had always known of but previously had been afraid to talk about. Other officially historic non-events (non-events in the sense that they found no place in the history books) were now being discussed. The Mongolians were asking the Russians about another disappearance – that of a colossal gold-covered bronze statue of the many-armed Buddhist god Avalokitesvara which stood seventy-five feet high inside the great wood and brick Temple of Maidari in the compound of the Gandan monastery. The temple and statue had been erected as a monument to appease the gods when the syphilitic Living Buddha of Urga's sight began to fail. The statue, said to weigh almost 160 tonnes, had taken on the same national significance to the Mongolians as the Elgin Marbles have to the Greeks. The relic was rumoured to be in Leningrad somewhere, but many believed it had been melted down by the Soviets during the Second World War to make bullets.

Questions were also being asked about Mongolia's leaders during times past. Purges, personality cults and subsequent denunciation have been features of Communist regimes for as long as they have operated, and the Mongolian People's Revolutionary Party has been no exception in this sense. The umbilical link between Mongolia and Moscow has thrown up Mongolian equivalents of the leading characters of Soviet history. Sukhe Bator was Mongolia's Lenin, Stalin found a very able Mongolian counterpart in the form of a man named Choibalsan, and the Mongolian parallel to Brezhnev was a fellow called Tsendenbal. And just as Stalin and Brezhnev have been reassessed in recent times in the Soviet Union, so Choibalsan and Tsendenbal have come in for a bit of public scrutiny in the Mongolian People's Republic.

Choibalsan was one of Sukhe Bator's original team of revolutionaries who set the whole sorry tale of Communist rule in Mongolia in motion. He had been educated in a monastery until the age of seventeen, when he went to Urga to work in various odd jobs such as porter and nightwatchman. He taught himself Russian and became an interpreter and schoolteacher before becoming involved in revolutionary activities.

While being intimately involved in the 'Final Solution' of the 'religion problem' in the 1930s, Choibalsan rapidly rose to power, becoming Premier in 1939. He did so simply by liquidating most of his rivals on the way. The process owed much to what was going on in the Soviet Union. Stalin was essentially running the show from the Kremlin, and numerous sickly tributes to Stalin emanated from Ulan Bator, such as in 1932, when he was thanked for his 'openhearted and wise advice', presumably on how to set up a police state and institute a reign of terror over the Mongolian populace.

Stalinist purges became as common currency in Mongolia as in her friendly neighbourhood superpower. A real threat from Japan loomed over Mongolia, and thereby the Soviet Union in the 1930s and consequently Mongolian society was found to be riddled with Japanese-backed agents and saboteurs at every level. Naturally these people needed to be brought to justice and exterminated. But you did not need to be a Japanese conspirator to warrant a visit from the forces of the Internal Security Office and an invitation to attend one of their show trials. There were much more sinister crimes to be committed than the downfall of the State. The Party's Central Committee member in charge of State transport was found guilty of organising traffic accidents, a capital offence. A Minister of Education was convicted, among other crimes, of trying to destroy the Mongolian national script. This extraordinary charge may have had its basis in a brief period when it was thought that Mongolian ought to be written in the Roman alphabet. But the true nature of the evidence that this man was convicted and executed on is irrelevant, since most of such evidence was made up anyway. Indeed, just four years after this particular trial, it was officially decided to replace the old Mongolian script with the Russian Cyrillic alphabet, for obvious very practical reasons, as the Central Committee, headed by Choibalsan of course, said at the time:

> The further cultural development of the country can only succeed along the path of the strengthening of friendly relations with the peoples of the Soviet Union and the acquisition of the extraordinarily rich Russian culture.

The unfortunate Education Minister was just a little previous in his ideas, and had plumped for the wrong alphabet.

Although the bare bones of events in the 1930s are clear – many people lost their lives, usually on trumped-up charges – exhuming the real truth from the innumerable layers of falsehood perpetrated in the 'historical' records of the period is a tricky task. History tends to have been falsified, rewritten and revised. Although each revision may be a closer approximation of the true events, it is well-nigh impossible to know when a reasonable representation of the truth has been reached. At the same time that Khrushchev began to reveal a few of the facts about Stalin's dodgier practices in the Soviet Union, so Choibalsan was exposed to the wisdom of hindsight in Mongolia, and he was castigated for having built up a personality cult at the expense of the good name of the Party. Many of the show trials were admitted to have been just that, and a number of the offenders were slowly revealed to be victims of unfortunate events. But that was as far as that first re-examination of the time went. The fact that Choibalsan was responsible for exterminating fellow Mongolians, most of whom were members of Mongolia's inadequate reserve of educated and experienced men, was not dwelt on. It is still one of the extraordinary enigmas of modern Mongolian history that an underdeveloped country could rip itself apart in the service of an imported ideology, supporting its brutality with wholly fabricated evidence, and continue the self-deception until the political climate in another country allowed it to begin a partial refurbishment of the truth.

There is little doubt that Choibalsan was an evil bastard, but, strangely enough, he is not the figure that Mongolians today most love to hate. That privileged position is occupied by his successor Tsendenbal, Mongolia's Khrushchev. Although Choibalsan was guilty of directing some horrendous crimes on his country's people, it was Tsendenbal who attempted to commit an even worse one in the eyes of the average Mongolian. Choibalsan's one saving grace was that it was he who prevented Tsendenbal from carrying it through.

Tsendenbal took over as Premier from Choibalsan in 1952, when the latter passed away, and continued to run Mongolia for more than thirty years. But it was early in 1952, before the changeover at the top, that Tsendenbal suggested the ultimate no-no. He thought that maybe, since the Soviet Union was such a great place, Mongolia ought to be incorporated into it as a new Soviet Republic. In a sense it would have been a logical step to take, since for most purposes Mongolia may as well have been part of the USSR anyway. But Choibalsan vetoed the idea. Whether he secretly thought that it was quite a good one, but that Mongolia, or probably more importantly the Soviet Union, was not ready for such a move, will never be known. But either way, it was Choibalsan's intervention to curb the eagerness of his deputy that has put him in a less unfavourable light in the eyes of the ordinary Mongolian today.

Tsendenbal was relieved of his position in 1984, while on a trip to Moscow. He was married to a Russian, and with the post *il tod* revelations of the true nature of the Soviet attitude to Mongolia, Russians are loathed in Mongolia.

One of the early demands of the fledgling opposition

groups in the first few months of 1990 was for Tsendenbal to be brought back to Mongolia from his retirement dacha near Moscow to stand trial for his economic and political blunders. The potential embarrassment of such a trial was successfully averted by the Party because Tsendenbal was supposed to have lost his marbles among the pine trees of Moscow's environs. The old man's senility was aptly portrayed in a TV interview broadcast in Mongolia shortly before I arrived. Tsendenbal rambled and repeated himself in just the way a senile old twit is supposed to. But Mongolians were not impressed with the performance. It was widely rumoured that his wife, Anastasya, had injected her husband with a mind-bending drug just before the interview to give the desired effect. The crimes that Tsendenbal was to have stood trial for were those of allowing Mongolia to become too dependent upon the Soviet Union and running up a huge foreign debt of nearly ten billion roubles.

Several of the leading members of the Mongolian Democratic Party, the first opposition party to rise from the fledgling democracy movement, were, however, half-castes, either half Russian/half Mongolian or half Chinese/half Mongolian. Tsendenbal's legacy is that any prodigies from similar unholy alliances with neighbouring foreign powers were looked upon with suspicion by the Mongolian electorate.

This was not the only problem that the five new parties entering the election fray were up against. Many of them were sorely lacking in manpower and could not rely on a well-oiled election machine such as the Party had at its disposal. A simple lack of candidates was a major problem. Even in some of the Ulan Bator seats for the People's Great Hural, the ballot paper would have just one name to choose from. Sainu told me that this was the situation in his constituency, and since he did not support the old Party the only way he could participate in his country's first ever democratic elections would be by not voting.

The Communists had also done their best to make sure that the elections were truly democratic according to their definition of the word. Although they had agreed to play the game, they were not above moving the goalposts. In order to break up the opposition threat, the election procedure had been drawn up to take place in two stages. The first vote would have all candidates for a particular seat, and the top two from this round would go through to a second ballot. In this way the Communists could be sure of dividing and splitting the opposing forces. But, not to be outdone, the opposition combined into an alliance, so that in the second round the two names would be from the old Party and the alliance. But the opposition had not been able to combat effectively another decree the Communists had brought in. Whereas in the countryside the number of voters per seat in the People's Great Hural was set at 2,500, in the city there was one seat for every 10,000 voters. The fact that the Communists could be sure of a healthy vote for their party in the countryside and were slightly less sure of the outcome in the city had of course nothing to do with the matter.

There was in fact little doubt that the Communists would be returned to power. But, for the opposition, it was a case of *some* representation in government, plus the fact that their efforts had speeded up the pace of change. All the parties, including the old Party, had pledged to introduce a market economy and further liberalise the country and its society. Essentially the main difference between the Party and the opposition groups was in the speed of the proposed changes. The transition to a freer democratic society and a more open economy would continue. But, as the Deputy Foreign Minister was quoted as saying, 'Communists are not magicians, so things will not change overnight.'

Despite the manoeuvring, the elections would certainly be a change from the usual Communist process, one that somewhat belies the assertion that Communists are not in

181

command of magical forces. There has been a notable lack of comment from the authorities in all the newly-democratic former Communist countries about the downfall of what had previously been publicised as a perfect system. The report from the Mongolian Central Electoral Commission on the elections of 1977 is typical of the way things were done in the heady days of total Communist control.

The report began by pointing out that there were 354 constituencies in Mongolia. By an astonishing and reassuring coincidence, there were exactly 354 candidates in 1977. This heart-warming information is further bolstered by the fact that no less than 99.99 per cent of the registered voters turned out to express their preference, a turnout that the report calls 'an objective expression of socialist democracy', which says it all really. But that was not all the good news. Of the 99.99 per cent who appeared dutifully at the polling stations, no less than 99.99 per cent voted for the candidates. Fantastic. The report does not give any indication of how the handful of characters who did not vote for the candidates expressed themselves in this realisation of socialist democracy, but there can have been so few of them that it hardly matters. Infinitely more important is the point that the turnout and the voting were a totally apt reflection of the popularity of the winning party. In fact the Party was so popular that no other parties bothered even to put up any candidates at all.

This sort of consensus is not surprising. On the occasion of the seventieth birthday of Joseph Stalin, for example, the Mongolian Communist Party's Central Committee thoughtfully wrote a congratulatory letter to the great man, assuring him that his name was 'the banner of the working class for the triumph of the great ideas of Marxism-Leninism, peace and democracy', and so on. 641,223 Mongolians signed the letter, or so we are reliably informed in an official history of the period. 641,223 amounted to the entire electorate at the time. This showed that 'each adult inhabitant of the Mongolian People's Republic thus testified to his sense of love and deep gratitude to the USSR, the great Russian people, and the leader of progressive humanity throughout the world – J.V. Stalin'.

If, however, you might still entertain doubts about the veracity of this near-perfect democratic utopia, you need only continue reading the report on the 1977 election. The Central Electoral Commission, the body charged with supervising Mongolian elections, happily assures us in its report that:

> After reviewing the election results, the Central Electoral Commission has declared that the elections to the Mongolian People's Republic People's Great Hural were held in complete accordance with the requirements of the Mongolian People's Republic Constitution and its provisions on elections.

So, you see, everything really was as good as it seemed. And do not for one moment think that 1977 was a flash in the pan. The elections of 1969, 1973 and 1981, to name but three others, had exactly similar turnouts and candidate-to-seat ratios.

In the last few weeks running up to the historic elections of 1990, Ulan Bator slowly filled with Western journalists. The American contingent was further swelled by the fact that the US Secretary of State, James Baker, was also due to visit Mongolia. The foyers of the Hotels Ulan Bator and Bayangol were soon crawling with hacks. Jerry and Jim, the two Cable and Wireless men, had lunch each day in the Hotel Ulan Bator and were forever being pestered about possible stories. They related the day's events to me over dinner in the Boghd Khan valley each evening.

Late one afternoon, as I was driven back to the valley from a visit to Ulan Bator's market, I noticed that there seemed to be a lot more troops around than normal. Both Mongolian and some Russians, which was unusual. Since we had been told that James Baker and his entourage of advisers would be taking over our apartment block when they arrived, I assumed that these troop movements were part of some sort of preliminary training for his arrival. But as soon as Jim, the Scotsman, arrived for dinner he put me right.

'Haven't you heard?' he said eagerly. 'A Russian conscript has gone AWOL from one of the local barracks. He took his Kalashnikov, fifty rounds of ammunition and a dozen grenades and has disappeared into the hills. The whole Russian army are out there now trying to find him. They've got to get him before Baker arrives.'

Jim was annoyed that he had heard the news only that afternoon, after lunch. He had the perfect headline for all the journalists.

'*Russian Rambo Loose in Outer Mongolia*. They'll love it.'

A visiting journalist's job in Outer Mongolia is not an easy one. There are many frustrations, such as the impossibility of speaking to key people at a moment's notice or easily hiring a car.

I met Graham, a man from Reuters who had come up from Beijing to write some articles on Mongolia. He had been taken on the usual trips to a co-operative farm, a factory and so on, but he had found that any non-packaged information was very hard to come by. He had wandered round the streets of Ulan Bator to soak up the atmosphere and perhaps come across some interesting ideas.

As dusk was falling, he was walking near the State Circus when a rather large Mongolian approached him. The fellow chatted away, slurring somewhat due to the effects of *arkhi*, which was heavy on his breath. It soon became clear that the Mongolian was not simply passing the time of day. Like a good socialist, he thought he might do his bit for the redistribution of wealth. He wanted Graham's camera.

I should mention at this point that Graham was a bit of a weed. He was a slightly-built man, with mousy hair and a pronounced limp. Ulan Bator is not generally a dangerous place, but if I was thinking of taking up urban violence there, Graham would have been the ideal first victim.

The Mongolian grabbed the camera. The strap was round Graham's neck and a struggle ensued. Since the capitalist from Reuters was clearly not entering into the spirit of things, the Mongolian decided to ram home the quick lesson in socialist principles by also grabbing Graham's jacket, which was hung over his shoulders.

The Mongolian was several sizes bigger than the man from Reuters, and the jacket would obviously not have fitted him well, but never mind, there was a principle at stake here. The next thing that Graham knew he was on the ground beneath the Mongolian, who was busy twisting the arms of the jacket tighter round his neck.

Graham shouted. There were plenty of people passing, he told me later, but none took the slightest bit of notice. Cries of 'help' in English turned to screams for the police as the coat arms were twisted tighter and tighter. A group of youths gathered round. They did not seem interested in helping: here was a bit of action, a brief diversion from the usual pastime of throwing stones. All the time the arms were getting tighter and Graham was in real danger of passing out, when suddenly the assailant disappeared with the youths, and Graham was left to pick himself up from the dust and struggle home.

Both his camera and his jacket were left. It had obviously only been a practice run.

● ● ●

My visit to the Ulan Bator market had been depressing. Row upon row of weatherbeaten Mongolians sat on the ground in the sub-zero temperatures with their wares set out in front of them. One man had a small tin full of odd screws and nuts in various states of rustiness. Next to him sat a woman selling a pile of broken metal coat hangers. Another character sold rusty needles and various bits of thread. A small crowd had gathered around a man further up the row whose object of fascination was an antiquated electric record player with two cracked sides and the playing arm missing. There was no way it could have been any use, but it was certainly something that needed inspection. There were bent screwdrivers, broken buttons, biros that did not work and keys with no padlocks. At the end of this row sat a wizened old woman whose sole object of potential value was a gasket, carefully presented on a scrap of grubby silk rag.

I had been warned not to take my camera to this small market square tucked away in one of the *ger* settlements on the outskirts of Ulan Bator. Was it because the authorities did not want anyone to publicise the sorry state of their country? And why was there a market for all this stuff that even in most underdeveloped countries would be left on the rubbish dump? You only had to visit any regular Mongolian shop to find the answer. It was simply because the chances of getting any of these bits of things, let alone a complete one, was virtually nil. In a way, Mongolia had the most concerted recycling system of any country I have seen.

The contrast of this miserable scene with the market of old Urga could not be more pronounced. The following account was written in 1921:

We entered the bazaar. The whole market was crowded. To the lively coloured groups of men buying, selling and shouting their wares, the bright streamers of Chinese cloth, the strings of pearls, the earrings and bracelets gave an air of endless festivity; while on another side buyers were feeling of live sheep to see whether they were fat or not, the butcher was cutting great pieces of mutton from the hanging carcasses and everywhere the sons of the plain were joking and jesting. The Mongolian women in their huge coiffures and heavy silver caps like saucers on their heads were admiring the variegated silk ribbons and long chains of coral beads; an imposing big Mongol attentively examined a small herd of splendid horses and bargained with the Mongol owner of the horses; a skinny, quick, black Tibetan, who had come to Urga to pray to the Living Buddha or, maybe, with a secret message from the other 'God' in Lhasa, squatted and bargained for an image of the Lotus Buddha carved in agate; in another corner a big crowd of Mongols and Buriats had collected and surrounded a Chinese merchant selling finely-painted snuff bottles of glass, crystal, porcelain, amethyst, jade, agate and nephrite, for one of which made of a greenish milky nephrite with regular brown veins running through it and carved with a dragon winding itself around a bevy of young damsels the merchant was demanding of his inquirers ten young oxen; and everywhere Buriats in their long red coats and small red caps embroidered with gold helped the Tartars in black overcoats and black velvet caps on the back of their heads to weave the pattern of this Oriental human tapestry. Lamas formed the common background for it all, as they wandered about in their yellow and red robes, with capes picturesquely thrown over their shoulders and caps of many forms, some like yellow mushrooms, others like the red Phrygian bonnets or old Greek helmets in red. They mingled with the crowd, chatting serenely and counting their rosaries, telling fortunes for those who would hear but chiefly searching out the rich Mongols whom they could cure or exploit by fortune telling, predictions or other mysteries of a city of 60,000

Lamas. Simultaneously religious and political espionage was being carried out. . . . Over the buildings around floated the Russian, Chinese and Mongolian national flags with a single one of the stars and stripes above a small shop in the market; while over the nearby tents and *yurtas* streamed the ribbons, the squares, the circles and triangles of the princes and private persons afflicted or dying from smallpox and leprosy. All were mingled and mixed in one bright mass strongly lighted by the sun. Occasionally one saw the soldiers of Baron Ungern rushing about in long blue coats; Mongols and Tibetans in red coats with yellow epaulets bearing the swastika of Jenghiz Khan and the initials of the Living Buddha; and Chinese soldiers from their detachment in the Mongolian army.

Today's market has had the colour and life drained from it. Jewellery and handicrafts have disappeared because they were bourgeois; livestock and meat are no longer to be found because the State is in charge and consequently there are constant shortages; the lamas have been exterminated and their practices destroyed, and the international traders are banned because they are no longer welcome. The heirs of the sons of the plain have been reduced to a miserable existence in a featureless society. Now that the worst aspects of the imported ideology responsible for this *reductio ad absurdum* have at last been thrown off, Mongolians once more have the opportunity to nurture their culture and identity back to life. It will take time, but the process has begun.

· 11 ·

GENGHIS RIDES AGAIN

An anticipatory hush fell over the crowd after the loud-speaker announcement, followed by a sharp intake of breath which quickly broke into unbridled cheers as the horsemen entered to a stirring trumpet herald. Deep, booming music reminiscent of a forgotten age filled the small amphitheatre with a haunting atmosphere, transporting the crowd back across the centuries. The mounted warriors poured into the stadium through the entrance as if it were a time tunnel unleashing a flood of seven-hundred-year-old history to surge into the present. Their capes were flying and their metal helmets and shields glinted in the midday sun. They were Genghis Khan's hordes riding again in the twentieth century.

Sainu and I had fought hard to get into the stadium for the opening ceremony of *Naadam*, part of the National Day celebrations. All the combatants were grimly clutching their tickets and elbowing, kicking and shoving their way to the entrance. Somehow in the excitement they had all forgotten the etiquette of queuing. I had to hold my cameras high above my head and be carried by the throng. And these horsemen dressed like Genghis Khan's hordes were not what I had been expecting. Neither had the crowd, to judge from their ecstatic reception. The occasion had an air of stunned delight.

'I have never seen sights like this before,' said Sainu, shaking his head in disbelief as the horsemen galloped round the small running track inside the stadium. 'The festival really has national character now.'

The crowd rose to its feet and clapped as the figures from their mighty past rode by. Cheers and whistles and shouts rang out and small children were held high. The ridepast exactly reflected the mood of the country in one poignant moment of national pride. Mongolia seemed to be collectively breathing a huge sigh of relief at being able to rediscover its powerful heritage, and to once more be proud of the memory of a birthright which had been for so long repressed and forbidden.

As we had squeezed into our places on the wooden bench, the acting President had arrived in the stadium. To everyone's amazement and obvious satisfaction, he wore a light blue silk *del* tied with a brilliant orange sash. It was the first time that anyone could remember a President dressed in anything but a stiff Western suit emblazoned with socialist enamel badges and medals.

The National Day celebrations are held to remember that day in 1921 when Sukhe Bator pulled off the Revolution and Mongolia embarked upon its course of socialist development. Ever since, the events of the public holiday have been a homage to the Soviet Union, with displays of gymnasts and orchestrated red flag waving. Here then, without any forewarning, was a National Day with a real Mongolian flavour.

The crowd could not get enough of it. The horsemen rode round and round in the midday sun. The horses surged forward like a tide of nature, the warriors moving in harmony with their mounts whose flanks shone. Everyone wanted this moment to last as long as possible. They had, after all, been waiting sixty-nine years for it.

Finally the horde swept out of the stadium through the time tunnel and back into the imaginations of Mongolians, but the feeling of pride remained and the atmosphere inside the stadium was electric. The next display was an entrance by a smaller pack of horsemen. This time they represented Sukhe Bator and his small band of revolutionaries riding into Mongolia to set up a socialist state. The leading horseman carried a banner with the dove of peace on it. The timing was poor. After Genghis Khan, Sukhe Bator was very much an also-ran.

But the Genghis theme was by no means exhausted. In the centre of the sports field sat a large round two-tier podium stuck with nine poles. Hung from the top of each pole was a series of dangling white things representing white horses' tails. It was Genghis Khan's standard, symbolic both of the great khan himself and his empire and also his Shamanic protective deity. The standard remained the focal point for the rest of the opening ceremony. Legions of men and women in national dress flooded the field and did a bit of synchronised dancing, each one bowing to the nine-tailed standard.

Then several hundred wrestlers appeared from all directions wearing the traditional wrestling costume which consists of heavy patterned leather boots, a pair of small knickers or trunks and a very brief long-sleeved frontless jacket in red or blue. Most of them were man-mountains who looked as if they could throw a yak over a *ger*. They entered the grassy arena with their arms extended in a bizarre birdlike strut. It was a strange spectacle: fifty tonnes of solid Mongolian brawn, all doing charade impressions for *Where Eagles Dare*. Each had his name read out, and at that point he performed his slow motion flap towards the standard and touched his forehead to the base.

The wrestling competition began. It was to last throughout the three days of celebrations. The wrestlers are divided into two groups and fight in pairs in a round robin knockout tournament. Winners are progressively matched together and losers eliminated. By the end of the third day, the final two contestants would be left to wrestle for the honour of ultimate champion.

When the tournament started, a dozen bouts were set in motion around the playing field. There is no set ring in which the matches take place, but the winner is the one who keeps his feet. When one of the wrestlers touches the ground with his knee or elbow he has lost. Each wrestling pair was overseen by two referees, older men dressed in ceremonial silk *dels* and pointed silk hats. It was their job to hold the contestant's hat if he had one and to proclaim the winner, who then slaps his thighs and sets off like a slow motion eagle to fly round Genghis Khan's standard and enjoy the applause from the crowd.

After a few bouts Sainu and I left the stadium to drive out of town to Good Deed Hill, the finishing place for a series of horse races that were being held for the National Day celebrations. We felt slightly out of place walking towards the finish line, since most of the spectators were on horseback. We had arrived in time for the end of the stallions' race which had started earlier that morning and had been run over a twenty-five kilometre course.

Shaven-headed soldiers and militiamen in peaked hats patrolled the ropes that cordoned off the crowd. There were two tiers of spectators: rows of horses' heads patiently gazing over the ropes at shoulder height and, above them, lines of men and women who sat on the horses' backs smoking cigarettes and debating the outcome of the race. We pushed our way to a spot in front of a row of horses, which gently nudged us in our backs as we stood waiting for the first riders.

The jockeys were aged between five and ten years. As the leading pack appeared on the horizon, trailing plumes of dust in their wake, I could pick out the children through my binoculars. They were dressed in brightly coloured silk capes in reds, greens, fluorescent oranges and yellows. The girls' hair was tied back in flowing pigtails bound with red and blue bows. Nearly all the boys had shaven heads which gave them a grim look of determination as they whipped their mounts towards the finishing line. An antiquated tanker drove slowly along the run-in, spraying the ground with water to keep the dust down. It was an extraordinary sight: immense stallions being handled by kids, whose years had not yet reached double figures, but who looked as if they had been born in the saddle, which no doubt many of them had. Apparently some Mongolian children learn to ride at the same time as learning to walk. A particular cheer went up for one finishing rider who was just three years old.

As the stallions were galloping in, a murmur went through the crowd. A small boy dressed in a red tunic and a bright blue headband had fallen from his horse just three hundred yards from the finish. The boy burst into tears as he picked himself up from the ground and looked at his mount. The horse lay where it had collapsed under him. There was not a sign of movement. Suddenly the boy started kicking the horse in the chest with all his might. Two men from the crowd pushed him aside to continue the rain of kicks on the horse's breast. I was horrified, but Sainu explained that this was a well-known method for reviving collapsed horses when all else fails. The water-spraying lorry was driven to the scene and doused the poor creature, but it was all to no avail. The horse lay there, its sweat-sodden hide glistening in the sun, and a small crowd gathered to inspect the former mount of rider number 255.

After the race, the crowd broke up and milled around on horseback, chatting and laughing and inspecting the stallions. Fathers of the junior jockeys were busy scraping the sweat from the racehorses and flicking it to the ground with flat wooden sticks. A couple of men on the back of a lorry were doing a roaring trade selling soft drinks to the mounted spectators. Another man had sat himself down in the middle of the crowd to fill a long thin pipe with tobacco from a pouch he pulled from his *del* after the excitement of the race. Viewed from one direction, the backdrop was green hills and blue sky; turn round, and the colourful riders and spectators were in front of a sprawl of power stations and faceless apartment blocks snuggling in a haze of pollution.

The next race would be tomorrow, when many of the same three hundred or so children would ride four-year-olds over a thirty-five kilometre course. They breed children tough in Mongolia.

Our next event was the archery, the third of Mongolia's traditional 'three manly sports'. We jumped into the Mercedes and drove rather conspicuously back towards town. The archery took place in its own small stadium which was open at one end. The archers lined up at the open end and shot their arrows out across the grass towards the targets which consisted of a line of small leather cylinders on the ground. A hit was greeted by several characters standing by the target who raised their arms and sang a short ceremonial wailing song of praise which dates back to the days of Genghis Khan.

Each archer, dressed in silk *del* and pointed hat, had four arrows attached to his belt just below their heavy bone heads. The arm holding the bow was protected by a ribbon wound tightly around the sleeve to protect against the impact of the bowstring. When his turn comes, the archer tightens the bow in a horizontal position and then brings it up vertically to shoot.

Although the bow-and-arrow has been replaced by the gun as the basic weapon of the Mongolian steppes, it has not been gone for so long that all the legends about fantastic archers and their achievements have disappeared, as Owen Lattimore, in his book of *Mongol Journeys*, relates:

He had an old white, bad-good, nothing-particular

horse. One day someone came in from the pasture and said to the old man's son: 'A wolf has eaten that white horse of your father's.'

'No, you're fooling!'

'It's a fact.'

So the son went and told his father.

'Ah? What? Ah?' For the old man was deaf as well as nearly blind.

'A wolf has eaten that old nothing-particular horse of yours.'

'No, you're fooling!'

'No, it's the truth!'

'No, it's impossible! There is no wolf that would eat my horse. It doesn't exist.'

'Well, your white horse is dead, it's a wolf that's eaten it.'

'Indeed, yes; yes, indeed!' And the old man thought a long time. 'I shall look and see,' he said. He had his son help him to the door of his tent, and he held back his head and lifted back his eyelids. 'I have thought of it! That was not a wolf of the Khangai. That wolf came from the Altai. The Khangai wolves wouldn't eat my white horse. That is a white wolf from the Altai, as big as a horse. He will come back and eat some more. Did he eat the chest?'

'No, he only ate the hindquarters.'

'He will come back for the rest. Tomorrow morning you get up early and go out to the dead horse and watch for that wolf and tell me what he is like and what he does.'

So in the morning the son got up early and went out to the dead horse. Nothing came and nothing happened. 'That old man is very old and knows nothing.' And he was turning to go home when – here comes a white horse from the west. It came very fast, and it was not a white horse but a white wolf, as big as a horse. It finished eating the horse and went away to the west.

Over a range and down; over a second range and down; over a third range and out of sight. It could be seen no longer. The son went home and told his father.

'I shall get that white wolf! Bring me my bow and string it!' That was a joke, wasn't it? They all laughed. The wolf was gone, over three ranges and out of sight. But the old man demanded his bow, and the son brought it to him and strung it and helped the old man to the door, and the old man stood outside and held back his head and lifted up his eyelids.

'I see! What direction did you say?'

'West, and over three ranges and out of sight.'

'West? Well, turn me in the right direction!' So the son turned the old man – he was seventy-eight – in the right direction, and the old man pulled the bowstring back and back and back and let the arrow fly. Then he held back his head and lifted up his eyelids. 'All right!' he said. 'Now send a mounted man – two mounted men – over three ranges and bring back that wolf!'

Well, that was a joke. They couldn't send mounted men on an errand like that. So when the old man asked: 'Have the mounted men gone?' they answered 'Yes, yes!' But nobody went. But several days later a neighbour came in visiting, and they were exchanging word of the beautiful and the strange, and the neighbour said: 'They've found a great white wolf as big as a horse. Somebody shot him.' Then they sent out and fetched him in! The old man's arrow had gone over three ranges and into unseen places and hit him in the back of the neck, at the base of the skull, and the arrow came out into his jaws.

The ubiquitous marmot also has a close link to archery. According to ancient Mongolian tradition there were twelve suns around when the world was first becoming the world. Various things happened to the multiple suns, leaving just one. Several were shot by a hero called Tarbagan Bator, or Marmot Hero, who was an expert archer. When Tarbagan Bator died he became a marmot, and now a Mongolian may shoot a marmot with a gun but never with a bow and arrow.

Archery and riding were of course the two fundamental skills of the Mongolian nomad, the ones that enabled Genghis Khan to conquer his Empire. The *Naadam* events clearly demonstrated that these skills were still very dear to the Mongolians. An account written in the twelfth century by the Chinese observer P'eng Ta-ya reads:

> When their children are very young they are bound with a cloth on a board which is then tied to the horses and they ride with their mothers on horseback. By the age of three, they are bound in the saddle in such a way that they may follow the others. At four or five years of age they are given their own little bows and arrows. As they grow older they follow the hunt in all four seasons. . . . They gallop like the wind and their force is as a mountain avalanche. They can turn freely from left to right like a bird on the wing. As they gallop along they can shoot to the left even though they are facing to the right and this they do without holding on to the reins or saddle.

These skills were second nature to Mongolians since they were learnt from the very earliest age. And their military application was constantly practised during the time of the Empire in mass hunts which were carried out like military exercises. Tales of these hunts relate how they were conducted over huge areas, sometimes several thousands of square kilometres. Generals were given units to patrol and survey for wildlife before joining together in an enormous circle of troops, maintained with high precision, to close in on the game. Generals and commanders were responsible for any animals that might escape and were severely punished in such an event, sometimes with death. When the circle had driven the animals into an area of some fifteen kilometres in perimeter, the hunt would begin. Genghis Khan, and later his successors, would open the hunt, followed by the generals, commanders and their subordinates, each according to rank. The slaughter of animals would last for several days and when finished the game was counted and each hunter would receive his share.

In battle, these skills were combined with extraordinary hardiness and speed of movement. In emergencies, troops could march for ten days without any cooked food, living off supplies of sun-dried curdled milk which was dissolved in water to make a syrup. In cases of dire need the Mongolian cavalryman would open his horse's jugular vein, suck blood out and close the wound. Distances of 700 kilometres could be travelled in a fortnight, and if necessary 300 kilometres could be marched in three days. Each man had at least one reserve horse, and sometimes three or four. When moving fast like this, the men often slept in the saddle as they rode.

On the final day of the *Naadam* we were back in the stadium for the closing ceremony, the presentation of prizes and the final bouts of the wrestling. As we walked in, some of the wrestlers were being presented to the crowd and they began their thigh-slapping and eagle-flapping routines. Behind them the survivors were still locked in combat, but the ones who had been knocked out were wrestlers who had reached certain stages in the competition and thus had attained certain honoured ranks. A falcon is the lowest grade and so on up to elephants, while the very best, the lions, were still hard at it. A wrestler who twice becomes absolute champion is a titan.

A warm round of applause went up as the winning child jockeys entered the stadium led by older men in packs of five on their horses. The kids still wore their brightly-coloured racing gear and looked somewhat nervous as well as tired. The bright sunshine of the previous days had given way to cold and driving rain but the crowd were still warm with enthusiasm. The children were paraded to the front of the President's stand where a special song of praise was sung for the winner and his or her horse in each race. Then a bowl of victory *airag* was half drunk by the winning child riders and the remainder poured over the crupper at the back of the saddle in a ceremonious gesture.

Meanwhile the very last bout of the wrestling had begun between the two largest, meanest-looking Mongolians I had ever seen. Their struggle went on for an hour and a half. It was one of the most boring finals I have witnessed in any sport. The two wrestlers spent long portions of the time seemingly leaning on each other, punctuated by an occasional burst of activity every twenty minutes or so. The rain was steadily falling and the temperature was getting decidedly chilly, but the two man-mountains just stood there propping each other up, looking tired and dejected. It was a game of endurance in which the winner would be the one who lasted longest before getting bored and cold. Eventually it ended much in the manner that it had been played throughout. One of the men performed a very straightforward trip and the other found himself on his backside. The crowd roared, and the two wrestlers were applauded up the steps to be congratulated by the President.

Sainu and I dashed through the rain, which was now coming down in sheets, to the Mercedes, only to find that the driver was nowhere to be seen. After a miserable half hour, during which we stood outside the main stand with rain dripping down our necks, the driver appeared, full of apologies. He had stayed on to discuss the final wrestling bout with some friends and he went through the entire fight with Sainu on the drive back to the Boghd Khan valley. I was amazed that he could find so much to say about a ninety minute period in which almost nothing had happened, but Sainu assured me that the fight had been a constant battle of nerves and tactics which to the expert was of great interest. I had to concede that the finer points of Mongolian freestyle wrestling had completely passed over my head.

• ● •

The atmosphere of carefree partying during the three-day celebrations had been a contrast to the feeling I had experienced three years before during the May Day parade and public holiday of 1987. I had been looking forward to the parade in Sukhe Bator Square which evidently was to be a stage-managed homage to the Soviet Union and all the great things it stood for: peace, friendship, goodness, love. For several weeks before the big event I had been able to monitor the preparations on my daily walks across Sukhe Bator Square to the Hydrometeorology Institute. Large white marker lines and numbers had been freshly painted on the cracking tarmac to indicate where various parts of the crowd were to be positioned. Parties of school children in red bows and scarves and groups of bored workers had faithfully turned up carrying red flags for practice sessions in which a lone figure stood on top of the People's Great Hural building with a megaphone and screamed instructions at them about when to wave their flags and where to troop off in various directions. National flags and huge full-face portraits of the Politburo were draped from buildings, and graphic images of po-faced workers clutching various farming and industrial implements were put up all around the square. It all seemed to be building up to a particularly sickly tribute to socialism which should not be missed.

Unfortunately I did miss it. Even though the Hotel Ulan Bator was within spitting distance of the square, Bulcsu and I had been misinformed about the starting time. We awoke and had a leisurely breakfast, thinking the parade was starting at eleven o'clock. At just after ten we wandered the hundred yards or so to the square, only to find that the entire parade had passed by without us. Bulcsu was delighted because he had not wanted to see it anyway, but I felt rather miffed.

We strolled down to the park on the edge of the city and found that the big wheel, a present from the Hungarian Communist Party, was working. Lines of Mongolians, slightly blue from the vicious wind that whipped through the valley, were queueing for rides. We joined it and managed a whirl before the cold got to us and we retired for an early lunch of schnitzel in the hotel dining room. I had discovered a sachet of Aeroflot mustard which livened it up, so we did not feel completely left out of the celebrations.

We were slumped in my room after lunch wondering what we should do with the rest of May Day now that we had missed all the excitement, when the telephone rang. It was my minder and interpreter at the time, a man named Sod. He wanted to know whether we would be interested in seeing the events taking place that afternoon in the stadium because he had some tickets.

Sod had a wry sense of humour. On one occasion when he and I were poring over a paper on soil erosion, we came across a sentence estimating the quantity of soil lost from Mongolia across the border to China. Sod smiled after he had translated the phrase and said: 'They didn't must have visa.' But in the early days he toed the line and wasted time by asking me questions like: 'What is your opinion of Marxism-Leninism?' and: 'What is your opinion of the contradictions of the capitalist system?' He had a sidekick called Chimbat, a soil scientist from the geography department. Chimbat was also a good man, as it turned out, but Bulcsu and I rather cruelly nicknamed him 'Bastard' in the first week and it stuck.

We met Sod and Bastard on the steps of the hotel. The wind was even stronger than it had been in the morning and it soon became so cold that I had trouble speaking because my mouth felt like it had just had a local anaesthetic. Small flakes of snow were now being hurled along in the gale and they stung the face like tiny missiles. Sod wore a light mackintosh and a fedora hat while Bastard wore just an open windcheater. They laughed when we told them how cold we felt.

'Middleton, this is nothing,' Sod quipped as we marched across Sukhe Bator Square. 'Come next time in winter and then you really will feel cold.'

On the far side of the square sat a building with a large portrait of Batman and another of Gorbachev outside on a hoarding. Bulcsu asked Sod what the building was.

'This is Lenin Club.'

'What goes on there?' I asked.

'Cultural activities, Soviet films.'

'Who can go in there?' Bulcsu asked, smelling a rat.

'All people.' There was a pause.

'All people?'

'Mongolians not allowed in here, or only by invitation, because if they all came there would not be enough room.'

'That's socialism for you,' said Bulcsu with disgust, but Sod did not answer.

When we reached the stadium there was a small crowd milling around in the biting gale. Sod made with the tickets and we entered the concrete stand. There were some wrestling bouts going on and Sod explained the basic rules. The sparse crowd seemed absorbed, the sky was blue as ever, behind the stadium white apartment blocks stood like skeletal bee hives for the workers, and the temperature seemed to be dropping all the time.

The wrestling finished with some eagle-dancing round a red flag at the side of the grassy arena, and the next event came on. A group of schoolgirls mounted a podium and sang traditional Mongolian songs into a loudspeaker system that allowed every fourth word through the high-pitched feedback screams. This was greeted with a short round of applause. By this time my bottom had become part of the concrete bench and I could not feel my toes. Next came the Mongolian People's Militia rock band, five guys in grey uniforms and peaked caps complete with guitars, drums and keyboards. They tested the mikes, tuned up to the feedback screeching and launched into the first number. This was getting to be surreal. I asked what they were singing about, and the answer came back: 'World peace'. I pinched myself. We sat through six songs, by which time I was seriously worried that I was going to get frostbite. All I could feel were my hands which I kept beating against my legs, the ones with two pairs of trousers on against the cold, but with little effect.

I suggested to Sod that perhaps I had had enough, but he told me to wait because I would really appreciate the next event. Some people were setting up a podium on the grass as the Mongolian People's Militia rock band began to pack away their guitars. Other men were erecting a large tractor tyre, a wall and some ramps. It seemed to be an obstacle course of some kind. Below us four soldiers appeared. Each man was dragged forward by three of the largest, meanest, most vicious-looking Alsatian dogs I had ever seen. The beasts had muzzles drawn tight over their jaws.

'Now there will be a performance by the spy-catching dogs,' Sod said with just the hint of a smile.

I looked at Bulcsu and immediately we came to the same conclusion: this was the time to leave. A few drips of adrenalin limped through my body and I was able to stand. Although I was well-nigh frozen solid, I was sure that this would be little disincentive to the beasts in charge of counter-espionage. One soldier was no match for three spy-catching dogs when they had the smell of Western capitalists in their nostrils.

• ● •

The evening after the final day of *Naadam*, I had been invited to a rock concert at Sukhe Bator Square's new Cultural Palace, a monstrous modern pile that had been constructed between my two visits. I had only taken the invitation half seriously when asked by a vivacious and rather attractive Indonesian woman who worked at the Ulan Bator office of the United Nations Development Programme. Sainu was not terribly convinced when I told him.

'What rock concert?' he asked. He had not heard of one.

The Cultural Palace turned out to be a veritable maze of mostly closed doors and unhelpful people on some sort of duty doing nothing much other than talking to their friends who were also doing nothing much. None of these people had a clue about any rock concert. I began to feel that this was, after all, a ridiculous request. Mongolia had changed, it was true, but for there to be a rock concert in the Cultural Palace just four months after the Politburo had resigned was asking a bit much. My resolve began to waver and I was about to tell Sainu not to bother, when he said: 'This man says it is in here.'

A crowd of young Mongolians were squashed up against a glass door which was firmly shut. On the other side of the door stood several usher-type people looking unconcerned. The concert had started. I had missed it. Sainu, however, did not give up so easily. He forged his way through the crowd to the door and motioned to a man who looked as if he might be in charge to open it and speak to him. The door was opened a fraction, which was the man's mistake. He valiantly tried to keep it at just a fraction while Sainu explained. The man relented and decided to let us through, which was the signal for half the mêlée to crush through with us.

We made our way with twenty extra bodies upstairs to the auditorium and filed in to stand along the walls. It was a small theatre seating perhaps 300 people. On stage was a man dressed in black leather. He wore a biker's jacket covered in studs, a thin white scarf, skin-tight black trousers and black gloves. He was midway through a version of *Rock Around the Clock*.

The concert consisted of a series of one-off acts and songs, which, other than *Rock Around the Clock*, were mostly Mongolian. A stunning young woman in a long white dress and long black silky hair came on to rapturous applause, followed by what can only be described as a Mongolian Jimmy Osmond, a very confident boy of about twelve wearing a pink jumpsuit who gave a magnificent performance with a guitar, reminiscent of Elvis Presley.

Many of the songs sung that night had particular significance for the new democratic times. Rock music had played an important role in the transition from a one-party state. At the end of 1989 a group of journalists had got together to form a band and sing their own songs about the need for political change. Their band, *Honch*, or 'Bell', had become hugely popular, both perfectly catching and engendering the mood of the times.

The final song was their best-known. The stage was cleared and the lights dimmed. The haunting sound of Buddhist horns echoed through the auditorium, and my spine began to tingle. The spotlight fell on the man who had been singing *Rock Around the Clock* when I had first arrived. He entered from stage left carrying a bowl of incense. Gone were the leathers, studs and sequins; he wore a long flowing *del*. Another spot picked up a large portrait of Genghis Khan on the back wall and the man moved slowly in front of the picture, bowing low to offer the smouldering incense bowl in homage to the portrait of the greatest-ever Mongolian. Guitars and keyboards took over from the horns and he began to sing. The song, entitled *Let Us Apologise*, began with the words: 'We had no chance to say your name, you were a great man, sorry, it is our shame.' The chorus, a harmonious chanting of the man's name, '*Chinggis Khan*', reverberated through the crowd.

· 12 ·

GOODBYE TO GOOD DEED HILL

Before I left Mongolia in 1987, I persuaded Bulcsu to accompany me on the Trans-Siberian Express. He had no wish to see the Soviet Union, he said, but the thought of entrusting his life to Aeroflot again had even less appeal.

Reserving a place, buying a ticket and obtaining the various transit visas through the Soviet Union and Eastern Europe presented an awesome series of bureaucratic hurdles. The reservations and ticket purchase had to be made under the user-hostile auspices of *Zhuulchin*, and the visas involved an endless succession of visits to Embassy officials, most of whom showed no interest whatsoever in doing their jobs. The only exception was the Hungarian Embassy, to which we went in desperation at the last minute because our forms for Polish and East German visas had still not been processed by the eve of our departure, three weeks after our application. We had an advantage here, of course, in that Bulcsu could speak

Hungarian, and the delighted attaché celebrated our application for two of his visas with a large bottle of peach brandy.

A week before our departure, I suddenly became *persona non grata*. The Mongolian authorities stopped paying for me. I was told to leave five days before my tickets could get me out.

I approached the British Embassy with my problem.

'You're up a gum tree, old chum,' I was told.

There was no chance of catching the Trans-Siberian earlier since it was completely booked up, so despondently I made my way to the Aeroflot offices with Sod to see whether I could bring my plane ticket forward. Luckily for me all the flights were booked solid, so I could after all catch the train. But I had to vacate my room in the Hotel Ulan Bator. There was nowhere else to go. The nights still produced several degrees of frost so I did not fancy sleeping rough, which would probably have resulted in arrest and imprisonment anyway.

Sod and I sat down in the hotel dining room to mull over the problem, and we ordered mutton soup. In any normal country there would have been a cheap hotel that I could have holed up in or someone would have offered to put me up for the intervening period. Sod apologised that he could not do this for me; it would be the obvious solution, he said, but it was not possible.

The mutton soup arrived and Sod tucked in. After picking out the huge chunks of white fat from my bowl, I was left with three pieces of rubbery meat and some slices of carrot floating in a thin broth. I told Sod that in the West, fat was thought to give you heart disease. Sod had heard of this crazy idea. He said:

'With fat no is there big problem. My arteries very wide. Without fat I cannot eat.'

I eventually slept on the floor in Bulcsu's room.

The Trans-Siberian is a long train ride. The reason is that Siberia is big. A glance out of the window as the train pulls out of Novosibirsk, and it's hard to imagine 3,000 kilometres of flat nothingness before the Arctic Circle. How can any train cross seven time zones? Our compartment was a surreal womb rushing us through one of the most hostile environments on earth. Often I wondered during our four days crossing this place just how anyone could live somewhere that is frozen solid for eight months of the year and a mosquito-ridden swamp for the rest.

There was quite a send-off committee at Ulan Bator station to wave us farewell. Norbu and one of his friends from the student hostel, Bastard, and even Lamujab turned out. As we climbed out of the taxi a dust devil swept up the road and swirled across the assembled crowd. The train pulled out on time at ten to two, and Bulcsu produced a bottle of Cinzano from his bag.

The train trundled northward. We passed through Darchan, an industrial city with not a *ger* in sight. Just outside the sprawl of factories, a ruined temple lay beneath a hillside on which the words *Let Peace Continue* had been spelled out in white stones.

Continuing peace was not uppermost in the minds of the customs men at the Mongolian border town of Sukhe Bator. When they opened the door to our compartment we could see the look of delight that came over their faces. They gave their undivided attention to the contents of Bulcsu's baggage. After forty minutes they had confiscated seven books, including a much-treasured three-volume dictionary of old Mongolian that had been given to Bulcsu as a present.

It was dark outside as we pulled out of Sukhe Bator, Bulcsu and I smoking heavily to relieve the tension, much to the annoyance of our carriage's attendant since it was strictly a no-smoking compartment. The train creaked its way through the night across no man's land and into the

Soviet Union. A floodlit siding awaited our arrival at Naushki for the Soviet version of the same rigmarole. It was 11 p.m. and a fine drizzle was beginning to fall.

Kids fresh out of military school, their uniforms still starched stiff, dealt with our passports and checked over the compartment with a torch and stepladder, looking for stowaways. Who would ever want to stow away *into* the Soviet Union, I thought to myself. Then the customs arrived, and it was my turn. The man in charge had breath that reeked of alcohol and a face on loan from a warthog, with short black greasy hair. He smiled as if he was about to sell me a secondhand car.

'You speak Russian?' he asked. I did not. Slowly he turned the pages of my passport. 'Post-grad-you-ate-stew-dent,' he read.

'That's right.'

His eyes twinkled and he moved his head closer, positioning it as he might have done if his breath had contained a truth drug.

'Narcotics,' he whispered. It was a statement.

I shook my head. 'No.'

Every item in my suitcase was pulled out and inspected in great detail. Then the two men left, and I was halfway through repacking my case, cursing as I went, when they returned with four of their friends and the whole process started all over again. Our compartment, designed for two people and really only big enough for three when standing up in a row, resembled the famous stateroom scene in one of the Marx Brothers' films. Bulcsu was relegated to stand in the corridor while I crouched on one of the seats and the six Soviet customs men climbed over each other to inspect the contents of my suitcase and bags. I kept wanting to produce a klaxon from my coat and sound it, ordering two hard-boiled eggs.

We had our first sight of Lake Baikal at seven the next morning. It was frozen solid. The train hugged the shoreline for several hours and eventually, as we neared Irkutsk, the ice had thawed and the famous crystal waters became visible. Lake Baikal is renowned for several things: containing a fifth of all the planet's fresh water, its amazing abundance of endemic species of plants and animals, its particularly clear waters, and the fact that pollution from the numerous wood-processing mills on its banks have brought this unique natural feature to the brink of destruction. After we had passed through Irkutsk and stopped for the regulation twelve minutes, we rolled past miles and miles of heavy industry, petrochemical plants and power stations, and a man came along our carriage selling smoked sturgeon in little tin trays.

After Irkutsk the swamp took over. Endless hours passed of the same view: marshy ground sprouting with hummocks of grass, silver birch trees, muddy tracks to quaint wooden houses with corrugated iron roofs, and plots of agricultural land.

Some of the best swamp was at a place called Kargat. Apart from the few hundred yards of station platform, there appeared to be no firm ground anywhere in this sizeable town. The bog came up to the front doors of the chocolate box houses.

Snow was falling on the soggy fields, sprinkling them with white powder. Bulcsu and I sat in the restaurant car eating hot bortsch and steamed sausage.

At Zima, there was no platform, just a wide patch of wasteground before the station building. Black coal dust covered everything, giving the place a soft but dreary feeling. A line of *babushkas* was ready for the train, each standing behind a pram. The prams were packed with neatly-tied bundles of radishes and spring onions, home-made chutney in Bulgarian jamjars, and boiled potatoes in hard grey paper. There was a rush of passengers from

211

the carriages when the train pulled to a halt and the ladies with teacosies on their heads did a brisk business. While inspecting the women's wares I kept looking over my shoulder in case a goods train rolled into view. We had passed some of the gigantic trains that ply the Trans-Siberian route. These beasts are so long they can take half an hour to pass through a station, and if you are caught on the wrong side of them you are cut off from the Express and it will leave you behind in a godforsaken place like Zima.

Bulcsu and I were the only Westerners on the train, and at each stop two militiamen in heavy topcoats and peaked caps took up position alongside our carriage. More swamp. Another million birch trees. They did not let us off at Achinsk. It was a big place on a river a hundred yards across. The meander scars had cut cliffs three hundred feet high. Barabinsk was a floodlit goods yard surrounded by snow and swamp. The air was strewn with overhead wires. Several huge locomotives rested on their tracks, humming as the electricity pulsed through their veins as if they were some weird species of high-voltage beast. Voices over the loudspeakers gave the place an Orwellian atmosphere. A sorry crowd of shaven-headed prisoners would not have looked out of place. It was good to leave after our eleven minutes were up.

Tumen had an overpowering grey concrete station building complete with remote control TV camera looking towards the Ulan Bator–Moscow train and the two rigid greatcoats positioned outside our compartment. A group of skinheads in leather jackets and dirty jeans was hanging around on the platform looking very mean. They turned out to be conscripts and were lined up in front of the concrete monolith and marched away. A man from Novosti Press who was returning after a three-year posting in Mongolia started chatting to us on the platform and told us to look out for the pancakes at Sverdlovsk.

When we arrived at Sverdlovsk, the last Siberian stop,

there were no pancakes, but there was still quite a lot of bog around the city.

• ● •

Four and a half days on a train does funny things to you. The monotony of the scenery was tedious but never boring. Bulcsu and I would sit back on either side of the window in our compartment for hours on end without speaking, just marvelling at such an inhospitable and endless nothingness.

But at the same time we went slightly doolally in our berths on our own. We developed a game on the theme of 'I Spy', which we called 'I think with my little mind', which involved reminiscing about Mongolia. Then, because we thought that it was Saturday and in England the FA Cup final was being played, we spent ninety minutes giving each other a live commentary on our imaginary match between a Coventry City eleven full of Mongolian all-stars and a Soviet all-star team representing Tottenham Hotspur. To our amazement, when we returned we had got the final score correct, although our game had been played on a Friday. Not all our match statistics corresponded with the real thing however. The Boghd Khan scored a hat-trick, and Stalin was sent off for a particularly dirty foul on Genghis Khan.

Somehow along the way we had gained a day.

• ● •

In 1990, I left Mongolia by way of Beijing.

My last day in the valley of the Boghd Khan was spent with Sainu and Tserendeleg and another English-speaking

213

man from the Environmental Organisation sorting out the details of the trip for British adventure tourists that I would lead the following year. Tserendeleg took a typically bureaucratic approach and wanted us to produce a protocol which we could all sign. I devised a route based on the places that Sainu and I had visited and we settled on what the Organisation was to provide. We had a couple of toasts with a bottle of *arkhi* to celebrate reaching that stage.

Then came the question of prices.

'How much will this cost you to set up?' I asked Tserendeleg. The answer came back through Sainu.

'How much would you like to pay?'

It was difficult to say, I told them, since I had to balance out other costs: the trip was to include two days in Moscow, the trans-Siberian journey and the onward trip to Beijing. If they told me how much it would cost them, then we could add a percentage for their organisation and we would all be happy.

'You are a good negotiator,' Tserendeleg told me. I replied that I only wanted to make a deal that was beneficial to everyone. But they still refused to come up with a quotation.

'OK,' I said at last, 'how does sixty dollars a day per person sound?' I knew that this would be too little.

They went into a huddle and came out laughing.

'Perhaps the tour company can provide us with some Toyota Land Cruisers,' Tserendeleg suggested. 'You know how uncomfortable the jeeps can be, and we want our guests to be as happy as possible.'

The negotiating continued and we eventually arrived at a price which they seemed to be happy with. We had another toast. Then I pointed out that the tour company would offer tourists the option of sleeping in single rooms in hotels. This would be an extra charge, so could they tell me how much. Tserendeleg came straight back on that one.

'These people will be our guests, we can pay.'

'No, no, you don't understand, they will expect to pay more to have a single room.'

'They are our guests, it is our responsibility to accommodate them as they wish, if they want a single room we will provide it.'

This continued for a whole hour. I impressed upon Tserendeleg that an extra charge was expected. But he would not budge. Mongolian hospitality dictated that they as hosts should do their best to make their guests happy. I gave up trying to persuade them and just told them that they would be paid extra for each single room, and there was no further argument. Another slug of arkhi hit the backs of our throats.

The sun was shining brilliantly in the land of the blue eternal heaven the next morning as I climbed into the Mercedes for the last time and bid my farewell to the Boghd Khan valley. Ulan Bator had the feel of the morning after the night before as we drove through the empty streets. In Sukhe Bator Square a group of workers in riding boots and felt hats was taking down one of the banners that had been hung for the National Day celebrations. It depicted four smiling characters from various walks of life who stood in front of a modern cityscape below the slogan, 'We can build a human socialist society with workers' hammers, farmers' spades, herdsmen's whips and intellectuals' pens.'

The car purred through the industrial quarter, past the shiny metal tubes that ran along the road and the fat chimneys with ladders running up their sides. We swung out across the bridge by the huge pepper grinder cooling towers and sped out towards Good Deed Hill.

The flight to Beijing takes just over an hour, and the journey into the city at the other end takes almost as long. The streets of China's capital were chaotic in a gentle sort of way. Flying Pigeon bicycles flowed *en masse* like amoebas with their bells constantly tinkling. My taxi cut its way through the pedalling throng and swerved overdramatically to avoid pedestrians crossing the wide roadways. Heavy lorries belching thick black exhaust clouds and buses that bent in their concertina-middles plied their steady straight courses. At crossroads, traffic policemen in white uniforms and matching white gloves and face masks controlled the seething flow of humanity.

I walked from my hotel to Tiananmen Square. I was struck by the sea of flat faces all around me and the unattractive habit of the women in wearing ankle- or knee-length flesh-coloured stocking socks.

A young fellow started talking to me. He had just knocked off from his job at the nearby Kentucky Fried Chicken. He would show me round Tiananmen Square, he said. He asked me my name and when I returned the question he paused and said that he would like his English name to be Wilson. He could not really explain why.

Tiananmen Square was vast. It was full of people flying kites, and the atmosphere felt very gentle. Wilson asked if I would like to see the tank tracks left after the previous June's authoritarian response to popular demands for change to the system, and we walked over to look at the chipped steps around the Monument to the People's Heroes. Far off across the square the huge portrait of Chairman Mao looked on from his position in front of the Working People's Cultural Palace.

'How do people feel about what happened?' I asked him.

Wilson shrugged. 'We tried,' he said, 'but the system is very powerful.'

The following day I took a bus tour to the Ming tombs and the Great Wall. Half the population of China had turned out to scramble up the renovated section of wall at Badaling Pass. I paused at the top of a rise to gaze at the construction that snaked its way across the hills into the distance. The Great Wall was supposedly built to keep the Mongolian hordes at bay.

A sharp pinch on my thigh woke me from my reverie. I turned to see a small girl standing with her hands to her face to suppress the giggles. On either side of her stood a friend, also laughing. The three girls all wore blue tracksuits and plastic sandals. I smiled at them and they disappeared into the crowd.

AFTERWORD

All the former Communist countries that threw the system out in the late 1980s have found the going tough since. Mongolia is no exception. Like a junkie trying to kick the habit, the Mongolians are suffering a period of 'cold turkey' in which things are getting worse before they get better. Price rises and acute shortages of fuel and food have hit the country hard.

When I returned to Mongolia in the summer of 1991 to lead the first group of adventure tourists, the Mongolian Association for the Conservation of Nature and Environment was dispatching teams to former Soviet military camps to assess the environmental damage. Sainu, my interpreter, had left the association and was working in a new private import-export company. His largest customers were the Japanese. Anou, his friend from Moscow days, was mourning the death of her father who passed away in somewhat mysterious circumstances the morning after attending a cocktail party at the Russian Embassy. Former

President Tsendenbal had also cashed in his chips, peacefully in his sleep in his Moscow dacha.

Ulan Bator still looked much the same, although some more of the hoardings depicting Lenin and his goatee beard had disappeared and there were rumours that the city's name would revert to the old Urga. A spanking new glass-fronted hotel promising international five-star standards was under construction. Russian advisers were being replaced with Japanese entrepreneurs, American businessmen and Peace Corps volunteers.

Norbu, the Tibetan student, was nearing the end of his studies at the University. Along with all Mongolians, he held his breath during the short-lived coup in Moscow in August 1991, but he must have been overjoyed a month later when the Dalai Lama visited Mongolia.

INDEX

Index

221

Index